PATTERNS OF THE FANTASTIC II

STARMONT STUDIES IN LITERARY CRITICISM NO.3

Edited by

Donald M. Hassler

☆ STARMONT HOUSE ☆
Mercer Island, Washington
1985

This book is dedicated to Professor John Hand of Columbia College in Missouri. He was scheduled to be on the academic program at ConStellation, but died August 4, 1983.

Library of Congress Cataloging in Publication Data:

ConStellation (1st : 1983 : Baltimore, Md.)
Patterns of the fantastic II.

(Starmont studies in literary criticism ; no. 3)
Selected papers presented at ConStellation (the 41st World Science Fiction Convention), held at Baltimore, Sept. 1-5, 1983.
1. Science fiction--Congresses. I. Hassler, Donald M. II. World Science Fiction Convention (41st : 1983 : Baltimore, Md.) III. Title. IV. Title: Patterns of the fantastic 2. V. Title: Patterns of the fantastic two. VI. Series.
PN3433.2.C65 1983 809.3'876 84-2683
ISBN 0-916732-88-6
ISBN 0-916732-87-8 (pbk.)

Published by Starmont House, Inc., P.O. Box 851, Mercer Island, WA 98040, USA. Printed in the United States of America. Cover design by Stephen E. Fabian.

First Edition---December, 1984

Preface

If it were not for the encouragement and support of Ted Dikty and Starmont House, of Julian May the novelist, of the Committee for the 41st World Science Fiction Convention, and of the officers of the Science Fiction Research Association this collection of essays would not have seen print. All but two of the essays (Merritt Abrash delivered his originally at the SFRA meeting in June where Rosemarie Arbur also read an earlier version of her essay) were first presented as papers during the academic programming track of Constellation in Baltimore. The 1983 Worldcon was, in fact, the second year for a unified programming track concerned with academic work on science fiction and fantasy; Patterns of the Fantastic II collects selected texts from that program. In addition, much valuable discussion was voiced by other writers and critics who participated in the program. Hal Clement, James Gunn, and Barry Malzberg made provocative contributions that are not collected here. Among the critics who shared in the program, but without printed texts, were Martin H. Greenberg, Elizabeth Anne Hull, Thomas William Hamilton, and Joe De Bolt. Finally, a highpoint of the program for which we also, unfortunately, have no text was the well attended panel discussion on Soviet Science Fiction that took place Sunday noon, September 4, 1983. The Soviet writer Eremey Parnov and the Soviet professor and translator Valentin Kotkin shared ideas with a lively audience at that crucial and tense moment in the history of our two countries.

For their hospitality and good organization, I wish to thank Michael Walsh, Peggy Rae Pavlat, and Jane Wagner of Constellation. I am indebted to Carl Yoke for helping with the early planning. My wife, Sue Hassler, advised and nurtured all along the way in planning and implementing this second academic track at a Worldcon. The Kent State University Research Council supported the typing of the book manuscript and some of my travel; and I wish to thank Dean Eugene Wenninger, in particular, for his support of the academic study of science fiction and fantasy in a time when budgets are lean and tastes tend to retrench. Lastly, my typist, Barbara Burner, is always skilled and patient with difficult words.

D. M. H.
February 22, 1984

Contents

Donald M. Hassler

Introduction--Dangerous Tastes: Science and Fiction

Each of the authors of the essays in this collection is (or has recently been) sheltered within the primarily contemplative world of the academic. Several are mathematicians or computer scientists; but most of us work in the humanities and, in fact, work with imaginative literature, or "fictions." A few years ago Hal Clement made a comment about us near the end of a long letter in Analog where he was discussing a question of chemistry raised about his novel The Nitrogen Fix (1980). Since I had just finished writing my Starmont volume on his work, the following words burned deep into my consciousness, "I am absolutely delighted to have a reviewer criticize a book on scientific grounds . . . ; I was beginning to fear that the English departments had taken over."[1] This collection is hardly a "take over." But it does represent the continuing and growing interest of academics--if not all English teachers--in the phenomenon of fictions grounded in the mythos of science.

Even more challenging, however, than a misunderstanding of our tastes by the writers of hard science fiction, who after all like any artists must maintain a kind of defensive amazement that they are being paid attention to in the first place, is the misunderstanding of science fiction by our colleagues in the academic study of the humanities. Perhaps it is the ever-shifting paradigms, the indeterminacy of modern science mirrored in the fictions, that make our taste for this popular literature suspect to the humanist. Furthermore, a key element in the academic enterprise of writing about science fiction is the theoretical attempt to understand the very relation of science and fiction; and this theorizing may seem presumptuous and out of place to our more traditional colleagues. (We hear complaints about commercialism, but I think rather it is the theoretic presumption that is the most dangerous element in our enterprise.)[2]

In fact, one reason that extended and non-traditional discussions of the literary nature of science fiction (such as the essays collected here) may be suspect in English departments themselves is that art and the meaning of art have tended to become the intellectual "fat cats" of the academic world. This is no doubt one reason Hal Clement is suspicious of English departments. In a real sense, all the battles have been won for the traditional view of art. For these fat cats, the meaing of the good and the true and the beautiful is self-evident, eternal, static, beyond any question, and thus entirely too closed and, paradoxically, unreal. In Frank Lentricchia's fine descriptive study of recent literary theory that encompasses the field from structuralism to deconstruction entitled After the New Criticism, Murray Krieger is the clearest advocate of this traditional view of art. Here are a few sentences about Krieger's ideas that I think capture the kind of "fat cat" self-satisfaction in the traditional view:

> . . . in an act of consciousness "unique" to the artist, an art object is "created" which, given our proper attention to it, will afford us a "unique" kind of human experience. Through this experience, somehow, we are to return--finally Krieger wants to break out of all the isolationist traps he has set for himself--to the human world somehow specially endowed, epistemologically freshened by an aesthetic experience, to perceive in a "unique" way, to enjoy "the unique view of the world which can come with the purely poetic experience."[3]

The quotations from Krieger suggest that he considers the poetic experience to be both exclusivist and somehow an almost "solid" and eternal entity in its own right. To be arch and a little disrespectful about it, the poetic experience for Krieger seems as solid as Dr. Johnson's famous stone or as self-evident as death and taxes.

Without making Krieger or Samuel Johnson out to be merely straw men, I have argued elsewhere that the real intellectual precursor of modern science fiction is David Hume.[4] And it is the fiction of indeterminacy in science fiction, I have argued, that permits us to theorize most provocatively about the nature of fiction itself and about the nature of reality. So these fictions about fictions collected here (as well as my work elsewhere) are, indeed, in a middle state. They are neither the fiction nor the science of science fiction itself; and they challenge academic assumptions about art--though some come closer to the traditional view than others (see Rosemarie Arbur's essay following).

Finally, although I can only speak for myself, I suspect most of us persist stubbornly in this middle state because we believe that "work" and "works" in literature should finally be what my friend and former president of the Science Fiction Research Association, Joe De Bolt, labeled for me last year following his trip to Russia as a prime literary characteristic of Soviet science fiction: "kind." Fictions that are "kind" (according to De Bolt's description and Charles N. Brown's comments at an SFRA seminar in June 1983) are fictions that promote good social values or good understanding. On the most practical level, then, science fiction may be at the cutting edge of social change, of epistemological understanding, and of the preparation for the future. It is possible, I think, that many of our academic colleagues have ignored any vision of the future in their commitment to traditional values; and so they resent our pushing at the edges of the traditional. In any case, the essays that follow are both academic in that they are made by people somewhat sheltered in the contemplative world and dangerously non-academic in that they want to engage shifting scientific understandings, technology, and the future.

Kent State University

Notes

[1]*Analog*, 101:13 (December 1981), 173.

[2]Much of the introduction is taken from an Honors Day talk I presented to the English Department at Kent State University in April 1983.

[3]Frank Lentricchia, *After the New Criticism*. (Chicago: University of Chicago Press, 1980), p. 218. The quotation marks refer to Krieger's text *The New Apologists for Poetry* (Minneapolis: University of Minnesota Press, 1956), p. 20.

[4]See my book *Comic Tones in Science Fiction: The Art of Compromise with Nature* (Westport, CT: Greenwood Press, 1982).

Merritt Abrash

The Hubris of Science: Wells' Time Traveller

The Time Traveller in H. G. Wells' The Time Machine is one of the most widely known characters in all science fiction, yet as a major fictional creation he is peculiarly incomplete. Although he is indisputably the central figure in the novel--the focus of the framing story as well as the hero-narrator of the visit to 802,701--only the barest of hints about his personal life (and nothing, of course, about his name) are provided. In fact, there doesn't seem to be any personal life--in his house in Richmond we see him in no situation, nor does a word escape his lips, that does not involve science in theory or action. Family? Biography? Hobbies? All are left blank.

Since there is practically no personality, it is hardly surprising that studies of The Time Machine have almost nothing to say about the Time Traveller as a person. For example, Mark Hennelly made a remarkable analysis of the Traveller's character in terms of its Eloi and Morlock aspects and their reconciliation[1] but this has little to do with the Traveller as a human being with a temperament, habits, fears, desires and all the other baggage we carry around as personal attributes, not social science abstractions. So what kind of man is the Traveller? We have a long story full of evidence, if we can figure out how to read it.

The portrait that emerges from the chapters at the Traveller's home is rather flat. He is earnest, humorless and not very patient with slower or less informed minds. Science is his only topic of conversation, and conversation seems to be the only entertainment at his dinners. Yet it is clear that he is an important man, sought after by substantial people. The Thursday night dinners are at his house; he has invented not only the time machine but chairs on which the guests are comfortably seated; and we have the narrator's word for it that the Traveller "was one of those men who are too clever to be believed; you never felt that you saw all round him; you always suspected some subtle reserve, some ingenuity in ambush, behind his lucid frankness."[2] No doubt about it--a man of exceptional competence who has earned the respect of all thinking people.

That is in Richmond, circa 1895. In 802,701, this same man projects an altogether different image. Intellectual forcefulness gives way to emotional changeability, methodical procedure is replaced by ill-considered impulse, and the supremely skilled man of science bungles everything he sets his hand to. The contrast is so striking that Wells had to be making a major point.

Consider the record of misaccomplishment compiled by the Time Traveller in 802,701. I am referring not to his inaccurate theories about humanity's history, but to his dunderheaded planning and action. Upon arrival, he starts out well by remembering to unscrew the machine's operating levers, and failing to keep an eye on the machine shouldn't be held against him considering the deceptive circumstances. But his reaction to the machine's disappearance is downright embarrassing. After a night of sheer hysteria, he deduces that the machine is in the White Sphinx' pedestal and proceeds to such unprofessional makeshifts as banging at the bronze doors with a stone and badgering the obviously unresponsive Eloi for information. He is aware of the need to gain the confidence of the Eloi in order to learn about his new world, but is unable to follow his own advice. His impatience and roughness scare them off; he rapidly gives up on their language (which, in its lack of abstract terms, strikes him as nearly useless in any case); and he even fails to draw intelligent conclusions from non-verbal messages such as Weena's fear of the dark. "I was still such a blockhead," (59) this supremely self-confident scientist confesses about this latter failure.

Then the Traveller becomes aware of the Morlocks, and his actions become almost bizarrely inappropriate. He descends into the Morlock realm, which a six-year old child would recognize as a hopeless trap, with nothing but four matches. Why only four matches? Because he had used up the rest of these irreplaceable items merely to amuse the Eloi--so much for judgment and foresight. He barely escapes the Morlocks, and can think of no more ingenious plan than to find himself a place he can fortify; then, however, his earlier glimpse of the seemingly unforgettable Palace of Green Porcelain chances to wander back into the memory of this master of keen observation. Although now understanding that moonless nights are the occasion for some great danger, he leaves for the palace--taking Weena with him--late in the day. He misjudges the distance by over fifty percent--a degree of incompetence ordinary non-scientific folk would find hard to match.

After spending the night safely on an open hill, this man to whom careful measurement is second nature completely loses track of the time at the Palace the next day, so the sun is already setting by the time they leave for home.

Sure enough, the Traveller misjudges how long it takes to get to the forest they must traverse, so it is completely dark when they reach it. Although he had correctly avoided going through the forest the previous night, now--for important reasons to be discussed later--he plunges in, after starting a fire at the edge to dazzle the Morlocks he knows to be about. It never occurs to him that he has no way of keeping on a straight route in the dark and that he is almost sure to fall asleep if they have to stop. He also seems unaware of the tendency of fires to spread through forests, which, as a scientific fact, are generally rich in combustible materials. Naturally Weena is soon seized by the Morlocks, although the Traveller is greatly comforted by the conviction that she is probably not eaten by the horrid creatures but merely burned to death by the fire he had set.

When he gets back to the White Sphinx, the pedestal doors are open. He immediately throws away his iron bar and relies wholly on the matches from the Palace--which turn out to be "the abominable kind that light only on the box" (89). Once again a fairly obvious thought has failed to occur to this mighty scientific mentality, and he is lucky to escape from the future world at all.

What are we to make of this extraordinary ineptitude, compounded of poor judgment, unstable temperament, lack of foresight and sheer incompetence? After all, no such shortcomings are even hinted at in the Richmond chapters, so they must have a deliberate relationship to the Traveller in the context of 802,701. But what?

A good place to start is with his lament when he finds the time machine missing. "At once, like a lash across the face, came the possibility of losing my own age, of being left helpless in this strange new world" (51). Helpless? But he is, from available evidence, by far the most powerful creature, both physically and intellectually, on earth. He might feel isolated, or bereft, but helpless? What an odd reaction! Why does the Traveller--a man of obvious courage and initiative--feel that way?

As mentioned earlier, Wells does not provide him with any particular personality or life outside of his profession. His status comes entirely from his identity as scientist. There is no sign of any other social role, nor does his dinner table badinage--lack of it, actually--suggest a personality which generates its own magnetism. To his friends, and in his way of life, the Traveller is an extraordinary scientist with no other observable attributes.[3]

What becomes immediately apparent to him in 802,701 is that his identity as scientist has no meaning there. The intimations of uncommon intelligence, profound understanding and practical impact which Wells' contemporaries associated with the image of the scientist are totally lost upon the Eloi. At best, the Traveller might be accepted as a magician (although the little people do not take magic any more seriously than they do science) but of the methodical use of the intelligence to produce effects in the external world vastly disproportionate to the raw capability of individual strength and will, the Eloi lack both experience and concept. The Traveller finds that the nimbus with which the mystique of science clothes him among the sophisticated Victorians is invisible to the childlike Eloi.

He finds himself, in fact, disarmed by the same paradox as a later Wells hero: Nunez, in "The Country of the Blind." Nunez' ability to see gives him a unique advantage over the sightless people taken singly or in small numbers, and of course he has a far greater range of knowledge than they. Yet he is completely helpless among them. The underlying cause is that they cooperate against him as a society, but initially--at the moment of the crucial first encounter--the explanation is psychological. If the valley people had any memory, even a legendary one, of sight and its powers, they would treat Nunez with a respect verging on reverence and acknowledge him to be superior. What renders Nunez powerless is precisely the fact that the valley people lack all concept of sight and therefore do _not_ respect it. His sightedness is reduced to a purely physical advantage without any mystique, and that is not enough.

Similarly, the Traveller, who has spent all his days in a society which continually reinforced the notion of the scientists' unique potency, suddenly finds himself stripped of this identity. His abilities are set at naught, because his scientific way of thought cannot connect up with anything in the experience of the Eloi. He can amuse them by lighting matches, but it is only a moment's diversion, not a portent of powers yet to be revealed. He cannot get coherent information out of them or organize them for any purpose, because the concept of orderly procedure has long since faded from the Eloi mentality. It turns out that his first reaction to the loss of the time machine was justified--he _is_ helpless, in the sense that there is no way he can project his scientific knowledge and abilities beyond the scale of his own unaided efforts.

And there is no other mode in which he can operate. Trying to deal with the Eloi in terms of casual human relationships lacking any common outlook or goal quickly exhausts his patience. Despite his own advice, he is unable "to be calm and patient, to learn the way of the people (53). . . . Face this world. Learn its ways, watch it. . . . In the end you will find clues to it all" (55). Oddly enough, it is the _discipline_ required by this seemingly random route to knowledge that defeats him: "I could work at a problem for years, but to wait inactive for twenty-four hours--that is another matter" (55). This inability, even when he is pressed by desperate circumstances, to shift from a narrowly intellectual way of thought to a looser human-based one points to a kind of cultural-evolutionary overspecialization--the scientific mentality as a maladaptation in any social environment that does not acknowledge its superior validity. That this was one of Wells' themes is further indicated by the dramatic change in the Traveller when, in the Palace of Green Porcelain, he finds himself among actual fragments of the world which had nourished him as a scientist.

The mere presence of mechanical apparatuses and

chemical substances sets off a huge surge of hubris in the Traveller. The acquisition of as trivial a collection of objects as matches, an iron bar and a lump of camphor fires him with total confidence that now he can master the Morlocks and recover the time machine from the pedestal. The Traveller acknowledges that the iron bar is the only tool he yet has for these tasks, "But now, with my growing knowledge, I felt very differently toward those bronze doors" (81).

What growing knowledge? It is not clear precisely what the Traveller is referring to, but certainly his information about the Morlocks is far too fragmentary to permit much confidence that an iron bar and some inflammable materials will place them at his mercy. Never mind, he has a tool, he has chemical aids, he has products of science, and he is ready to take on the world. Plunging into the dark forest so poorly armed is an act not of calculation, but of faith--the lump of camphor as church candle illuminating the bar of iron as icon, in the service of a God the Traveller refuses to admit is dead.

Another episode in the Palace is even more revealing of Wells' awareness of the hubris of science. The Traveller finds two dynamite cartridges in an air-tight case, but they turn out to be dummies. "I really believe that, had they not been so, I should have rushed off incontinently and blown Sphinx, bronze doors, and (as it proved) my chances of finding the Time Machine, all together into nonexistence" (80). This is the merest of passing reflections in the novel, but behind it stands a judgment of profound significance. The scientist, finding (discovering) a means capable of producing a desired effect in the world, immediately applies it without considering its broader consequences. To the Traveller's mentality, locked bronze doors + explosive power equals blasting through the doors. End of quotation. Only afterwards would he discover that the end (recovery of the machine) was incompatible with those means.

Hence the delicious irony of the Traveller eventually finding the bronze doors open without any effort on his part. Some disregarded self-counsel shortly after the machine's disappearance--"If you want your machine again you must leave that Sphinx alone" (55)--proves wiser (and more effective) than all his scientific calculations and pursuit of devices. The scientist's knowledge, Wells makes clear, is not to be equated with wisdom; in fact it is the very efficacy of that knowledge which tempts him into immoderate application.

With that, of course, we move into the shadows of Dr. Moreau on his namesake island and Griffin of _The Invisible Man_. There is scarcely any doubt of Wells' attitude toward _their_ scientific mentality. They are Evil Scientists through and through, self-isolated from their fellow humans and dreaming diseased dreams of truly hubristic scope. In contrast, the Traveller has a sentimental fondness (we hope that's all it is) for dear little Weena and displays no organized delusions of grandeur. Yet, no matter how much more acceptable a personality, he is at one with the scientific mentality of the others, sharing with them the assumption that the scientist, having placed his hands on a lever of superior power, need not hesitate to push it as far as it will go. What happens in these stories by Wells, in fact, is that the levers themselves, by how far they can go, become the scientist's standard of how far he should push them.

What Moreau and Griffin hope to do on a massive scale, by affecting human society and even biology, the Traveller does in a small, almost symbolic way, by taking Weena into the forest with little more than scientific mystique to sustain them. His hubris, small scale though it is, has the same result as his successors' gigantic schemes: suffering and death. Again, the Traveller's reaction to Weena's death is far more human than those of Moreau and Griffin to the pain they cause, but Weena, the most innocent of all, is dead all the same, no less a victim (if an indirect one) of a master scientist's disregard of limits.

But the ultimate victim of the hubris of science turns out to be the scientist himself--which, in the order of the universe, is as it should be. Moreau dies at the hands of a creature whose inherent nature he has scientifically violated, and Griffin at the hands of those he would rule through the amoral power of a scientific feat. And the Traveller? He, too, presumably perishes, and why not? Overconfident as always when in his scientific element, he sets off on his second journey almost as ill-equipped as on the first, when he was not even wearing decent shoes. Even after his harrowing experiences in the relatively benign 802,701, he leaves now with nothing but a knapsack--small enough to be carried under one arm--and a camera. No doubt there are lots of matches in the knapsack, and the shoes are the best money can buy (or perhaps his own invention).

But it is the mentality that matters, not the details. Wherever the time machine deposits him, the Traveller will continue to be a nineteenth-century scientist, supremely confident of the virtue of manipulating the material world, contemptuous of the unmethodical, and oblivious to ways of thought other than his own. If, as this suggests, *The Time Machine* is Wells' first and somewhat tentative fictional exploration of the danger posed by the scientific mentality, *The Island of Dr. Moreau* and *The Invisible Man* are not departures from *The Time Machine* but the full flowering of some of its themes. These early novels manifest a growing concern lest the scientist's strongest impact on society prove to lie beyond this invention or that discovery; in the Traveller's small knapsack, as in Griffin's small lodging or on Moreau's small island, there is plenty of room for the occupational hazard always lurking to translate disinterested knowledge into demonic use: the hubris of science.

Rensselaer Polytechnic Institute

Notes

[1]Mark M. Hennelly, Jr., "*The Time Machine*: A Romance of 'The Human Heart,'" *Extrapolation* 20 (Summer 1979), 154-67.

[2]H. G. Wells, *The Time Machine/The War of the Worlds* (Greenwich, Conn.: Fawcett, 1968), p. 32. Quotations will be followed within the text by page numbers from this edition.

[3]Many years later, in *The Shape of Things to Come* (New York: Macmillan, 1933), Wells elevated the contrast between the scientist's professional and personal attributes into a generalization: "The nineteenth-century scientific man had been a very lopsided man; often he had proved himself a poor conventional snob outside his particular investigations" (p. 264).

Rosemarie Arbur

Ars Scientia = Ars Poetica

The question I propose to address here is the old, basic, fundamental, and almost reflexive and redundant "Is science fiction about science?" By the end of my discussion, I shall have answered it with the equivalents of "yes, of course" and "most assuredly, no." But--I hope I make this clear as I go along--I do not expect to have contradicted myself, nor even to have confused the issue. I want to approach the question from the perspective offered by some literary theory so that I can try out some approaches to my hypothesis that science fiction has to have science in it because it is the literature of a "scientific" culture.

We are all aware of the monster called a Hidden Meaning. Almost all students hate English because of that monster introduced to them by former teachers. We are also aware of some quasi-literary entity called Theme ("so the theme of this story is . . ."), and we may be aware of Leigh Brackett's having designated it, with a proper sarcasm, the "Big Think." (She did not like people to pretend they were reading when what they were really doing was dredging for a Serious Message.) As far as I know, the monster called Hidden Meaning was brought to the study of literature by Boccaccio. Maybe he was just fooling, or maybe he was feeling guilty at having written such entertaining tales and so had to do penance, but he did write words to the effect that "hidden meanings" in literature are valuable in direct proportion to the effort required to dig them up. And then we have Leigh Brackett, telling us of:

> the vast glooms of interstellar space, where the great suns ride in splendor and the bright nebulae fling their veils of fire parsecs-long across the universe;

> where the Coal-sack and the Horsehead make patterns of black mystery, . . . and a billion nameless planets may harbor life-forms infinitely numerous and strange. Escape fiction? Yes, indeed! But . . . it was an escape into a reality which even now some people are still trying to fight off.[1]

I don't think she would have agreed with Boccaccio at all, nor do I think that any of us began our reading of science fiction with the notion that we would somehow get ourselves a Big Think, or a Theme, or a Hidden Meaning out of what we read.

But here I am, at a science fiction convention, saying things that are supposed to be somewhat "academic"; one problem I see--for people like myself--is that Deans and Department Heads will say "A Con? a what?" but will say nothing at all if I put a fun space opera on the rack of neostructuralist criteria they do not understand because . . . --well, professors just do things like that. But I do not like "hidden meanings" at all, and really do suspect that looking for them is a way to avoid looking at the real thing: in this case, real science fiction.

(Last spring, I read a review of a book of critical essays about science fiction; the reviewer reserved his strongest approbation for the chapters which I found the most esoteric. What upset me most about the review was the genuine high praise for an essay analogous to one on "Young Goodman Brown" in which the main point is to establish that the concavity in the "altar" rock is filled with amniotic fluid--so that there would be a balance between the symbolic values of the hollowed ("hallowed"?) rock and the flaming ("haloed"?) phallic pine trees in the immediate background.)

Almost at the beginning of this discussion, I indicated the hope that some old fashioned literary theory, if applied to science fiction, would get us out of the footnoted woods and make teaching and studying science fiction more simple and enjoyable. My "Goodman Brown" example shows sufficient reason for my hope. I mean: we who know better may not be harmed by playing around with the potential hidden meanings of the disfigured faces of Ged and Selver,[2] but when I told my students what Ursula Le Guin told me--that their cheeks were scarred because she is missing her left buttock--they did not get the joke; one young man, in fact, observed that Le Guin must not be able to walk "because the gluteus maximus is necessary for the articulation of the leg." After all, the publisher-an-arcane-article routine has messed up all too much appreciation of mundane literature; do we have to follow the same dreary path in our researches into science fiction?

Nationality affects response to literature. In Europe, Verne and Wells (and Huxley and Orwell) and Lem are generally thought to be "authors," whereas we Americans assign a special label, "science-fiction writers," to people like Silverberg and Vinge and Budrys and Le Guin and Dick and Wolfe and Cherryh. I shall oversimplify and be literally chauvinistic: "science fiction" has been an American kind of literature.

The reason for its being American is more complex than what I shall explain, but my oversimple reason is a valid one. During the mid-1920's two literary phenomena took place: I. A. Richards got "New Criticism" started (in Britain, but it really flowered here), and Hugo Gernsback got Amazing Stories to the newsstands. In the late thirties and during the forties, "New Criticism" became the academic thing to do, and the "Golden Age of Science Fiction"--the era of the pulps--arrived.

The generation fascinated by "scientifiction" found themselves in a world of promise; travel to the nearer planets would soon be commonplace and "atomic power" would meet every physical need. In contrast, the "image" projected by the typical New Critic was very nearly that of the unworldly professor at home in his ivory tower but very much a stranger to the everyday world that was reeling from the impact of scientific advances and technological complexities. Thus, despite the genuine literacy of people like Hamilton and Kuttner and Brackett and Bradbury-Weird Tales and Astounding were not The Sewanee Review. It did not matter that Kuttner and Hamilton spent some very long nights "just talking about" seventeenth-century English poetry. The pulps did not specialize in ironic, ambiguous poems, and the literary journals did not emphasize the importance of well-plotted stories with scientific verisimilitude.

Science fiction became a literary ghetto, at least in the United States. For whatever confluence of whatever reasons--one must be that science fiction had to do with new discoveries, fresh ideas, mechanical marvels, and all the rest--the "ghetto literature" remained truer than other literary forms to what is a quintessentially American literary tradition.

In May 1842, not even five years after Emerson proclaimed that "We have listened too long to the courtly muses of Europe,"[3] Edgar Allan Poe wrote a review of the Twice-Told Tales by Nathaniel Hawthorne, and in it defined and "invented" the short story as a specific and autonomous literary form.[4] That the literary expression of a self-consciously technological culture should meet the criteria for a new literary genre is, I think, more than coincidental. What Poe was writing about was not science fiction, but he was describing:

> that class of composition which, next to (the poem), should best fulfil the demands of high genius, . . . should offer (genius) the most advantageous field of exertion. . . . (He was describing) the prose tale, . . . the short prose narrative, requiring from a half-hour to one hour to one or two hours in its perusal. (The longer traditional novel) deprives itself, of course, of the immense force derivable from totality. Worldly interests intervening during the pauses of perusal, modify, annul, or counteract . . . the impressions of the book. But simple cessation in reading would, of itself, be sufficient to destroy the true unity. In the brief tale, however, the author is enabled to carry out the fulness of his

> intention, whatever it may be. During the hours of perusal the soul of the reader is at the writer's control. There are no external or extrinsic influences. . . . The idea of the tale has been presented unblemished, because undisturbed.

I am not suggesting that Poe was unconsciously laying the groundwork for the short stories and novelettes and novellas which became--and still are--the most usual published forms of science fiction. But I do suggest that the attributes of the short story are, in just the ways Poe describes them, exactly what the science-fiction narrative requires. Notice that "worldly interests" are held at bay, that the author of a short story can make the fiction "whatever it may be," that the "soul of the reader is at the writer's control," that "external or extrinsic influences" do not affect the "idea of the tale." These conditions are precisely those necessary for that "willing suspension of disbelief"[5] upon which all science fiction depends.

But it is not just Poe's "invention" of the short story which makes American literary theory especially applicable to science fiction. Walt Whitman, looking back on what is possibly the greatest period of American literature, wrote in "A Backward Glance o'er Travel'd Roads" (1888) that American literature had yet to come to terms with subjects he felt were especially American: "Modern science and democracy seem'd to be throwing out their challenge to (literature) to put them in its statements in contradistinction to the songs and myths of the past."

Himself a literary revolutionary, Whitman recognized that the writers who followed him in time would have to do more than acknowledge the tremendous changes which the end of the nineteenth century had ushered in. His own "Hurrah for positive science! long live exact demonstration!" was not enough, nor even his more specific mention (in the lines that follow that rather embarrassing one) of "the chemist," "the geologist," the person who "works with the scapel," and "the mathematician."[6] By 1888, Whitman realized that bits of his poetry like that quoted here, "made an attempt at such statements," but did not actually embody the new principles. "For all these new and evolutionary facts," he wrote of the challenge facing those makers of literature who would succeed him, new "meanings, purposes, new poetic messages, new forms and expressions, are inevitable."

Writing about what he saw in his "Backward Glance," Whitman could see in his own poetry the possible beginning of a literature that would break with the traditional "poems of the antique" in order "to conform with and build on the concrete realities and theories of the universe furnish'd by science, and henceforth the only irrefragable basis for anything." He saw in his own poetic attempts a hint of what literature had, in modern times, to embody: a "different relative attitude towards God, towards the objective universe, and still more . . . the quite changed attitude of the ego. . . . It is certainly time," he wrote in 1888, "for America, above all, to begin this readjustment; . . . for everything else has changed."

In these statements by Whitman there is the recognition that science and a different perspective on human life are going to become ever more prominent in American letters. In the assertions by Poe there is a blueprint for the best means to embody "the idea" in readable language. Further, there is the somewhat peculiar tallying of science and democracy in Whitman's view of the American future, a tallying that just may be peculiar to our American culture.

The democracy Whitman celebrates seems to be a principle which, when actualized, permits and encourages the greatest possible degree of individual freedom. The science he celebrates as well seems almost antithetical: as we learn more about how the cosmos behaves (above the subatomic level, anyway), we find greater constraints or scientific "laws" which limit freedom of behavior. Philosophically and even poetically, this apparent paradox is resolved as "liberty" becomes the ideal behavior of an entity that is so much itself that it is "unbound" by any influences not truly a part of its own nature. This ideal is very likely what Thoreau envisioned, as he formulated the principles of "Resistance to Civil Government": "'That government is best which governs not at all;' and when men are prepared for it, that is the kind of government which they shall have."[7] In other words, when we have socially evolved to the degree that we need not be ruled by anything but the true dictates of our human selves, we shall be ready for and indeed must live in perfect anarchy. This "anarchy," I suspect, is hardly the bogeyman of "social order," but rather the "anarchy" which can be said to "govern" the lives of intelligent animals who neither know nor are limited by any artificial laws.

Pragmatically, however, science and democracy become a dilemma. The more we learn about anything, the more we understand how it "obeys" the dictates of its nature. The human being, from a traditional American perspective, has the right to liberty as much as he or she has the right to life. By the turn of the twentieth century, writers were exploring the dilemma which Whitman suggested: our genetic background makes us what we are and forces us to do what we must do, yet this genetic heritage also gives us the ability to think about such "determinism," to conceptualize a life freed from it, and somehow to wrest qualities like liberty and perfectibility from scientific "law."

Poe's "blueprint" for an effective narrative is, at its most fundamental level, an apparently scientific prescription for the literary artist the end of which is not only a (freely) "preconceived effect" but a verbal artifact that embodies "invention, creation, imagination, (and) originality." Yes, a paradox? "here are the 'natural laws' of prose fiction which you, dear author, must follow if your tale is going to be original."[8] Poe celebrates originality, but he does so in language that reminds its readers of adherence to the almost scientific rules of syntax and logic. He tells us that

> originality (is) a trait which, in the literature of fiction, is positively worth all the rest. But the nature of originality, so far as regards its manifestation in letters, is but imperfectly understood. The inventive or original mind as frequently displays itself in novelty of tone as as in novelty of matter.

Unless I am guilty of woeful misreading, Poe here sets up the conditions under which the writer can treat the wonderful but hardly invented phenomena which are usually the object of scientific knowing as if they were "created" by the writer: by treating them linguistically so that they are apprehended by the reader as new, by writing about them in language remarkable for its unique or original tone.

Poe also clearly asserts that the aim of prose literature is truth:

> the tale has a point of superiority even over the poem . . .--the artificialities of (poetic) rhythm are an inseparable bar to the development of all points of thought or expression which have their basis in Truth. . . . Truth is often, and in very great degree, the aim of the tale. . . . Thus the field of (the story), if not in so elevated a region on the mountain of Mind, is a table-land of far vaster extent than the domain of the mere poem. Its products are . . . infinitely more numerous, and more appreciable by the mass of mankind.

Here, as if anticipating Whitman's realization that, "when everything else has changed," the forms proper to an American literature must be flexible, Poe extolls the prose tale as being almost infinitely adaptable. As if precognitive of Whitman's--and the future's--emphasis on democracy as a social ideal, Poe notes how the tale can speak to the largest of audiences. And, as if he had foreseen Whitman's--and others'--exaltation of science as an influence on American culture, Poe aims prose fiction toward the communication, revelation, and embodiment of truth.

Some imaginary centuries from now, an imaginary man will write his imaginary report "as if (he) told a story, for (he) was taught as a child on (his) homeworld that Truth is a matter of the imagination."[9] Genly Ai evidently thinks that "truth" is likely to be revealed most fully by a story of his experiences on Gethen: not a list of facts about the planet and its inhabitants, but a story molded by imagination. Genly Ai is the chief narrator of a novel. Because _The Left Hand of Darkness_ is a novel, not a short prose tale, we may expect that it has not one but several "effects" of the sort Poe describes as the ideal results of reading several tales, and our expectation is justified.

Even if one is able to read the novel at a single, leisurely sitting, it is too long and too various to have a single effect; it has several. Very likely, these include an experiential insight into the nature of trust and betrayal, an experiential realization that differences of culture and personality are likely to hinder accurate communication, an experiential shock that comes of encountering human beings who are sometimes male and sometimes female but never men and women, and an experiential sympathy for sapient beings who have no close biological relatives on their world and whose chief energies must be engaged in the struggle for survival on a planet so cold that a tiny ice-hammer is as necessary at mealtime as the cup that holds the beverage that freezes inside it.

This abbreviated list supports Poe's contention that the novel by its nature can produce neither a sense of "totality" nor achieve one single "effect." It also gives some sense of what The Left Hand of Darkness is about.

It is about "science." The Gethenians are the descendents of some proto-human stock that had evidently been altered to lack life-long sexual polarity; thus the novel is about the possibilities of genetic engineering, an offshoot of the science of biology. It is also about what is currently known as sociobiology: Gethenians do not know war, and the scientific observer (the reader) must explain the lack of large-scale, long-term violence in terms of "nature" (is war related to the effects of male hormones?) and of "nature" (they need not fight each other since they all must fight the deadly cold). It is about physics, too, and cryogenics, for the starship Ai had used to get to Gethen took 17 years, needing to obey the "law" that sets maximum velocity at lightspeed, and his companions in the ship "sleep" while Ai is living and aging as he does his Envoy's work. The physical anthropology in the novel determines that the Gethenians, like Earth peoples of the polar regions, have more subcutaneous fat than we do, and are shorter than we are so that they have relatively less body surface from which precious heat can radiate. And there is more.

Other works of science fiction contain even more "science." James P. Hogan's Inherit the Stars is an intellectual delight to readers familiar enough with paleontology, theories of cosmogenesis, geology, celestial mechanics, and similar subjects to be able to guess ahead of the narrative and decide how a 50,000-year-old human skeleton could have gotten on the Moon. Readers of Robert L. Forward's Dragon's Egg must be physicist-astronomers themselves to play a similar game, (the setting of the novel is the "surface" of a neutron star and its characters almost mass-less beings affected by electromagnetic fields as much as by gravity). Nevertheless, even ordinary readers have the opportunity to identify our concepts from the "evidence" presented by the tiny critters' experiences before the author makes it plain that they are contending with things like sunspots and solar flares. Hal Clement's novels and stories, some written much earlier than Hogan's or Forward's works, are at least equally enjoyable.

In one, "Fireproof," a saboteur manages to get inside an orbiting space station, and opens valves so that highly volatile fuel is available to demolish the station (it would seem) by just the spark from his cigarette lighter. But the manager of the station, talking casually with a less experienced and more officious member of the station's personnel, is fully aware of the saboteur's presence and intentions and, to the younger man's dismay, shows not a single sign of anxiety, even when hidden cameras show the ignition of globules of the dangerous fuel floating weightless in zero-gee. Some time prior to this critical moment, Clement's authorial narrative voice tells readers that anyone with a knowledge of high-school physics will understand the manager's nonchalance.

The story concludes, for the reader, twice. First, because the byproducts of combustion are water and carbon dioxide and because in an environment with no gravity there can be no convection, we see the saboteur's dismay when the "explosive" spheres of fuel he ignites burn quietly until the water and carbon dioxide smother the fire that produced them. Second, we hear the experienced manager of the space station offer a bit of advice to the man who hangs in mid-room still staring at the video screen that shows the pitiful results of the saboteur's mission. The manager explains the practical differences between gravity and no-gravity environments, one of which is the need to develop habits "such as always stopping within reach of a wall or other massive object." We smile, a bit chagrinned ourselves, to realize that by himself, the other man would hang "suspended helplessly in midair (all day,) out of reach of every sort of traction," for there's nothing he can grab to pull himself to floor or wall or door.[10]

Now, I could analyze this story point by point to show how nicely it fits Poe's criteria for the achievement of "totality," "effect," and "truth." But I do not mean to use the story here as that kind of "set piece." The reason I mention it is that, while it is totally dependent on physics (without the "science" there could be no story), the truth that it embodies has nothing to do with science at all. The story does inform us about the principles of combustion and gravity and inertia, but its true effect is dependent on "human nature." If, warned by Clement's authorial voice, we realize how the burning fuel is more dangerous because it's lost than because it's set aflame, we take delight in the station-master's practical superiority to the younger man who, in the excitement of the moment, has forgotten how things work in weightlessness. The stuffed-shirt's being deflated is an archetypal incident common to numerous stories set in numerous locales; people laugh at this archetype no matter what the guise in which it may appear.

Yet Clement is not satisfied with an accurate jab at inexperienced "authorities"; he ends the story with a man completely helpless in midair, and we readers as well as that character are chided mildly for not remembering that, in an environment without gravity, walls and doors and floors are as important as means of self-locomotion as they are as structural parts of any living space. We laugh first at the younger man's naivete about the fire; we laugh last about his and our own naivete about zero-gee. Poe's review insists that prose fiction have for its object "truth"; Hawthorne himself specifies Poe's claim, stating that a work of fiction--novel, romance, short story, or tale--"sins unpardonably so far as it may swerve aside from the truth of the human heart."[11] The "truth" that is important in Clement's story--and in any science fiction worth reading--is not the "truth" of fact or science. It is very much like the "Truth" that Genly Ai tells us "is a matter of the imagination." It is, as Hawthorne wrote more than a century ago, "the truth of the human heart."

Thus, I contend that Clement's and Forward's and Hogan's and Le Guin's works are about science--that science fiction is about science--but my stronger contention is that these and other works of science fiction are more fundamentally about the kind of truth that is not contained by the sum of the scientific disciplines. I am asserting that science fiction is "about" truth, the sort of truth that is accessible to any reader who is aware of the world we live in.

Just as literature is affected by nationality, it is determined to be what it is by the cultural context from which it arises. When I say that science fiction is about "the truth of the human heart" and then say that this truth is accessible to anyone aware of the world we live in, I am implying that contemporary science fiction requires readers to be conscious of the spirit of our time. And the spirit of our time, no matter how some people are kept in ignorance of it and how others seem to think that contemporary scientific "literacy" is unnecessary, is basically technological. We live in a post-industrial age. We live in a world transformed by applications of scientific knowledge and discoveries. If we refuse to admit these facts, we are intellectually lazy, or deficient in imagination, or just plain stupid. Perhaps we are stupid and unimaginative and lazy: the result is the same.

A "literary movement" is an attitude embodied in the literature of a culture that reflects some profound cultural change and the dominant responses to it. We are still under the influence of what we call the "Romantic Movement." American literature especially is either in some ways romantic or else (as in the late nineteenth century with the ascendance of "realism") anti-romantic. In either case, what values the Romantics extolled remain values sufficiently important that we must espouse them or condemn them; we cannot simply ignore them. So there was a Romantic Movement that arose systemically in Western culture: "back to nature" (because life in the industrial cities was so grim), and "hurray for the individual person" (because the "Industrial Revolution" was making people into machine-like parts of inhumane factories).

This Romantic Movement was followed by a swing toward a belief in progress (call it "Victorian" in England and "Realistic" in the United States). Of course, it's not quite so simple, for the "belief" raised certain "doubts," and the latter helped to produce *fin de siecle* literature overseas and "Naturalism" here at home. However it is qualified, there did exist a real consciousness of the impact of science on human lives. Science would save us, or, if it didn't, our miseries could be traced to a failure to survive as among the "fittest" in a world more and more aware of and influenced by scientific principles. One can even say that this post-romantic swing was itself romantic insofar as it romanticized Science.

Next came the cultural movement we live in today, a movement that has not been neatly named but nevertheless a movement that makes our age much more sophisticated than the last as far as knowledge of science goes, and much more mechanized because of really widespread applications of science. The application of science is technology, and technology and science fiction go hand in hand.

So here we are, with a literature (science fiction) growing out of a movement that is still romantic in some ways. If Nature was important to the Romantic because humankind's true place was within Nature's kingdom, Technology is important to us because humankind is now--because of the requirements of too large a global population--interdependent with technology if humankind is to have a future. (If humankind is to preclude its probable future, it is still interdependent with technology: once Trident II missiles go into production, we can terminate human civilization in only fifteen minutes, half the time it takes for the Soviet Union's land-based ICBMs to do the job.) Whatever name we wish to give the present cultural movement that dominates Western culture right now does not matter, for the movement exists and has been exerting its influence on literature for about half a century. The result has been a literary movement identifiable by the ascendance of science fiction, and "science fiction" the literary label brings us back to the basic question.

"Is science fiction about science?" The answer is "yes" if we take "science" literally as "knowledge," but it is certainly "no" if we understand "science" to mean what people learn in courses in physics and astronomy and geology and chemistry and that whole group of "subjects." Science fiction is literature, is narrative literature for the most part. And, as Poe and Hawthorne tell us correctly, that sort of literature is "about" truth.

Some time after Genly Ai was made to assert that "Truth is a matter of the imagination," Ursula Le Guin explained _The Left Hand of Darkness_ by saying that science fiction is actually a Gedankenexperiment, a kind of thought experiment analogous to those used by physicists: "Einstein shoots a light-ray through a moving elevator. . . . There is no elevator. . . . The experiment is performed, the question is asked, in the mind."[12] That Le Guin should describe a novel in a physicist's terms is appropriate, for her novel is one of many that arise from the literary movement I shall dare to name "Post-Atomic,"[13] the literary movement that results most often in literature called science fiction.

What is peculiar to science fiction is that, as literature, it readily assumes that humankind is now partly defined by its affinity for and dependence on technology, or applied science. Nonetheless, science fiction is literature, and literature is the use of language to embody truth and beauty. Since science fiction is for the most part prose narration, not lyric poetry, we can expect it to embody truth in language being used in an artistic way. This does not mean, however, that the result of having read a work of science fiction must be the understanding of a "truth" like that described by the universal law of gravitation. We must remember Hawthorne and our American literary heritage: "the truth of the human heart."

When someone asks if science fiction is about "science," the someone usually means "science" as in celestial mechanics or "science" as in the accurate integration of a number of facts. Now, because our culture is keenly aware of certain facts--like, one needs electricity if one's computer is going to function, one needs an operating cathode ray tube if one is going to be able to play a home video game--the literature that is science fiction cannot get away with not-facts. According to the article in Locus, Asimov went through his Foundation trilogy and changed every "atomic" to "nuclear";[14] he evidently did that because of a change in our knowledge of atomic physics. When he first started writing science fiction, he and everyone else could get away with "he held the blaster steadily, no longer fearing the alien who faced him." And the "he" who held the "blaster" could have been dressed in a cotton coverall and have been standing on the surface of Venus.

Readers won't tolerate that kind of not-fact in science fiction anymore, because it is about as untrue as having Neanderthals protecting their caves with crossbows in their hands. And the general knowledge of a science fiction reader today is sufficiently great--about "science"--that publishers are practically begging for "hard science fiction" novels and stories, and that a lot of writers have turned to fantasy so they do not, in their fictions, have to be careful not to alienate the reader by a blatant misrendering of scientific fact.

> "Is science fiction about science?"
>
> "Yes, if you mean 'Is there a lot of science in it?' There is more science in science fiction now than there ever was. There has to be; there is more science and technology in our lives now than ever before in the history of our species.
>
> "But that does not mean that science fiction is about science."

From a literary theoretical standpoint, the "science" in science fiction has become a necessary part of the literary element called setting. The more important elements of a literary narrative are the plot and the characters. So science fiction is still thought-experimentation about the nature of humankind. An earlier work of literature might start out with "a truth universally acknowledged, that a young man in possession of a fortune must be in search of a wife."[15] A work of literature appropriate to our own time might start, instead, with another truth almost universally acknowledged: that if there is going to be a permanent space-station / off-planet habitation, it is likely to orbit the Earth at the same mean distance as the Moon, only sixty degrees ahead of or behind the natural satellite.

> "But if science fiction isn't about science, then what is it about?"
>
> "What literature will always be about: 'the truth of the human heart,' or 'how human beings perceive truth,' or simply us."
>
> "Even when the action all takes place in a super-scientific artificial satellite?"
>
> "Especially then.

What that story is about is "us"--the characters who will react in certain ways if something blights the algae in their hydroponic tanks to the degree that food and oxygen will soon be in short supply. More specifically, the story will tell us how this or that particular character reacts.

If this space-station story is at least "fairly good," the protagonist is probably a likeable person, but with qualities and attitudes (these will in some way relate to the action) that differentiate her or him from "everyone." The language is exact and evocative: it gives the reader both a sense of being there and of feeling what the protagonist feels. There is some real urgency about what the protagonist has to do, and whatever it is needs to be problematic, so that the qualities of the main character are both developed and exhibited in her or his performance of some difficult actions. And, since this is a fairly good science-fiction story, the setting must be believable and rendered in however much detail is required for a sense of place and for the arena in which the protagonist is tested and succeeds (maybe fails) at the performance of the necessary action.

Now, that is a satisfactory description of the requirements of a fairly good science fiction story, but it is abstract. The problem that faces the protagonist has not, in my little synopsis, become clear or real. Let me try another "story."

Someplace in the township where my home is, one of the 418 worst toxic waste deposits in the country is located. I do not know where it is, because the Environmental Protection Agency isn't very specific. Most of the people in the township do not even know of the problem because most do not get the kinds of newsletters I do. All the preceding is true. Now, if I were to write a novel set in the vicinity of my home, if I were to perform a thoughtexperiment about how people react to poisons seeping ever closer to their wells, it might work. I think it would work better--there would be a better chance of my readers recognizing an important "truth"--if I set my novel on a colony planet, because "aesthetic distance" permits a truth to be accepted with far greater ease than does a "fictionalized account" of the facts.

Facts scare people, but good fiction entertains. ("Fiction" comes from the word for "making," and if I were to write a half-decent science fiction novel about the "truth" relating to those toxic wastes I would have to use the facts as well as the English language to make something that is a positive experience to read.) Further, if I moved my setting onto another world, I could exaggerate certain things without letting my story become unbelievable. My characters could be, because they are the sort who would make a years-long journey to a new world, a bit more courageous and probably a bit more educated than my real neighbors. The planet itself could remain exactly like this one, but I could use "imagination" to make the facts seem more like "truth."

That is to say, I would have to do plenty of homework--all kinds of research--in order to know the stability of the environment around my here-and-now home. Then, by making that environment exist on an imaginary planet, the fragility of ecological balances would almost automatically be emphasized. The fact that there is a silver ash uphill from my house--a tree that must be at least 300 years old--tells the intelligent reader that the groundwater is pretty much okay. For the ash, and for the huge willow in the back yard, it is: but we cannot have a well because U. S. Zinc has pumped the underground as dry as possible for mineshafts. Thus the members of my household are not so affected by that toxic waste because we have water brought in by truck, good water from a municipal system that had foresight long ago to buy lots of forested land in the nearby mountains. And, for most of the distance between the reservoirs and the city, the water is in underground conduits: once it's in the pipes, the acid rain and the particulate pollution cannot get to it. But I'd have to find out what the "pipes" are made of (probably cement and rocks with more-than-usual limestone, and that offsets the acidic influence of the ground minerals in the mountains).

I mentioned "the intelligent reader" some sentences ago. Well, he or she is the bottom line. At the present time, almost any work of fiction must have some elements of science or technology in its setting, and at the present time, anyone who claims to be literate should have some understanding of the physical facts of life in our technocracy. Some of you will gasp quietly at the fact that my drinking water is trucked in: that's right out of science fiction, right? Some others of you will not know why it's good to have a lot of limestone as the "bedrock" in the area where I live; well, there's lots that I don't know, but with acid rain a critical problem everywhere north and east of New York, I kind of think you should know about limestone.

Science fiction by virtue of the culture it arises from has much that is "science" or "technology" in it, but, as literature, its chief end is to communicate humanly meaningful truth. Right now, "science and technology" seem to many humanists crass or too complicated, or something, and these same humanists honestly look upon an electric typewriter as a necessary evil and--I find it very difficult to believe, but two professors married to each other and thirty seven years old are real-life examples!--a manual transmission something of a mechanical mystery. It is unfortunate that these persons still fall into the category "humanist," for they cannot understand much that is literally vital to human beings living in the United States at the end of the twentieth century.

Science fiction contains much that is literally vital to us. It may be simply imitative of the "real world" and thus have offices without typewriters but with keyboards (or "touchboards"!) connected electromagnetically to compilers and memories and CRTs. It may be metaphorically imitative of the "real world" in the way that _The Left Hand of Darkness_ is, relaying Truth by indirection, by the description of what human life without gender is, so that the reader may infer what he or she can about human life with gender. Paul Anderson's _The High Crusade_ is sheer nonsense, but it not only solves the problem of hiding from radar the mechanisms by which nuclear warheads are deployed; it also tells a large truth when it tells of knights on their destriers taking over spacecraft from some supersophisticated Aliens.

It may be that I am overcompensating: I can no longer read classical (or any other kind of) Latin passably, so I learn what I can from my students who are engineering physics majors (that's a five-year major, so don't be rude). In one science fiction course I was in charge of--I do not presume to say I was the only person teaching!--I made the regular course in science fiction a prerequisite, and then everybody read "Golden Age" science fiction and talked about how things have changed so that good science fiction is much harder to write, how various state-of-the-art technologies can be used in science fiction stories, and how much we all had yet to learn.

"Science fiction is about being truly human, as all literature is, except that it contains as parts of its setting and as agencies for its incidents a certain amount of 'science,' which functions to alert the reader to what humans need, metaphorically and literally, to learn."

Lehigh University

Notes

[1]"Introduction: Beyond Our Narrow Skies," The Best of Planet Stories #1 (New York: Ballantine Books, 1975), p. 3.

[2]Ged the protagonist of most of Le Guin's Earthsea Triology, Selver the Athshean "god" who brought war to his people in her Word For World Is Forest.

[3]Ralph Waldo Emerson, "The American Scholar" (as a speech, delivered at Harvard in August 1837), about one-third of the way into the last paragraph. It seems impractical to cite editions and pagination when the works I am quoting appear in most college-level American literature anthologies.

[4]Poe's 2nd review of Hawthorne's book, which appeared in Graham's Magazine, 20 (May 1842), 298-300. This essay is so important that I should like to locate exactly the sources of my quotations, but the essay is so widely reprinted--and sometimes in abridged versions--that referring even to the ordinals of the paragraphs might confuse more than clarify.

[5]S. T. Coleridge, a significant influence on Poe, coined the phrase in his Biographia Literaria (1817); it has become, for those who like neat phrases, second only to "sense of wonder" as a bench mark of science fiction and fantasy.

[6]Whitman's "Song of Myself," section 23.

[7]Quoted from the second sentence of the first paragraph of the essay identified correctly in the text (first published in 1849) but more commonly known as "Civil Disobedience."

[8]That "statement"--with my emphases--is my rendering of Poe's implicit and explicit advice; other uses of quotation marks indicate Poe's own language in his second review of Hawthorne's fiction.

[9]Ursula K. Le Guin, The Left Hand of Darkness, first sentence of Chapter 1.

[10]Earlier published in Clement's collection, Small Changes, quoted here from the paperback reprint: Space Lash (New York: Dell Books, 1969), p. 95.

[11]Emphasis added. Hawthorne's "Preface" to The House of the Seven Gables (1851), third sentence of the first paragraph.

[12]"Is Gender Necessary?" in Aurora: Beyond Equality, ed. Susan Janice Anderson and Vonda N. McIntyre (Greenwich CT: Fawcett Publications, Inc., 1976), p. 132.

[13]It would be nicer if the movement could be called simply "SF" but two letters--even with all they stand for and suggest--do not sound like a literary movement. I settle for "Post-Atomic," then, because it can be interpreted variously and yet accurately (after atomic theory was no longer a revolutionary hypothesis, after the detonation of the atomic fission bombs over two Japanese cities, after fission gave way to fusion as the power in the weapon of ultimate destruction, after lots and lots of people got around to realizing that nations as well as persons cannot stand on their own as separate entities (like "atoms"), and anyone is welcome to add to the list of congruent meanings).

[14]"Asimov's Bestselling Edge" in Focus, 15:12 (December 1982), n. 19.

[15]The famous first sentence of Jane Austen's Pride and Prejudice (1813).

Jared Lobdell

Thornton Wilder as Fantasist and the Science-Fiction Anti-Paradism: The Evidence of *The Skin of Our Teeth*

Before we can discuss what I am calling the science fiction anti-paradigm, it is necessary that we define the science fiction paradigm. I will call as witnesses three science-fiction writers and a fantasist--specifically Theodore Sturgeon, Isaac Asimov, James Blish, and Ursula K. Le Guin--before rounding off my discussion of the paradigm itself by appeal to a critic of science fiction, C. S. Lewis. With these I hope to set up my point of departure.

Sturgeon's view is that "A science-fiction story is a story built around human beings, with a human problem, and a human solution, which would not have happened without its scientific content."[1] Asimov's view is that "Science fiction is that branch of literature that deals with human responses to changes in the level of science and technology," backed by the additional statement that, in science fiction, "the surreal background . . . . could, conceivably, be derived from our own by appropriate changes in the level of science and technology."[2] Blish's Spenglerian assertion is that "Science fiction is the internal (intracultural) literary form taken by syncretism in the West" with its subject matter being that occult area where a science in decay overlaps the second religiousness."[3]

For Sturgeon, then, the problem of the story is brought about by science; for Asimov the human responses are responses to changes in the level of science or technology (extrapolating from our own present); for Blish, the subject matter--the material cause--of science fiction is science of the sort current in our age and its (Spenglerian) contemporaries. Let me leave the matter there for the present and go on to Le Guin on fantasy. Her tentative definition of science fiction as "the mythology of the modern world," followed by eight pages of qualification (largely because the definition is itself borrowed), is not very useful.[4] Better is her definition of science fiction as that subdivision of fantasy where "you get to make up the rules, but within limits. A science fiction story must not flout the evidence of science, must not . . . deny what is known to be known"--and it must, of course, like any fantasy, stick by the rules once they are set up.[5]

We can work with this--indeed, it differs in tone rather than in substance from the definitions of Sturgeon and Asimov: like theirs, it gives scientific extrapolation a determining place. Or at least, I should say, like Asimov's--between her view and Sturgeon's there is a divergence on inevitability: for him the story could not have occurred without scientific change, while for her science is the machine (in the old sense) and another machine might have done as well. That is why I call her a fantasist, but though she is, she recognizes that science fiction presupposes the laws of science as we know them. It is at this point she differs from Blish (at least in his later years), to whom the science of our science fiction is a branch of the occult.

Now Lewis would tell us that science fiction encompasses the Engineers' stories ("hard" science fiction), the Extrapolation stories where the point is in imagining "what it would be like if" (but with the caveat that these wear rapidly), the stories where science is a "machine" to get us to a set of circumstances necessary for a particular kind of story (his example being John Collier's _Tom's A-Cold_), the Eschatological stories whose purpose is speculation about the ultimate destiny of our species (H. G. Wells's _The Time Machine_, for example), the Mythopoetic stories where science is also a machine, in precisely the way Le Guin is speaking of it (and indeed this is the kind of story she is concentrating on)--and, of course, though in his view illegitimate, the subdivision we may call Space Opera.[6] The first three, and particularly the second and third, fit in with Sturgeon and Asimov (they being not the hardest of the "hard"), and with Blish, while--as noted--Ms Le Guin is chiefly concerned with the Mythopoetic, or at least with science fiction as a machine.

None of the critics or practitioners above deals with purely Eschatological science fiction, nor is it a particular concern of their definitions. Lewis's examples are _The Time Machine_, Arthur Clarke's _Childhood's End_, Olaf Stapledon's _Last and First Men_, J. B. S. Haldane's "depraved" chapter from _Possible Worlds_. I could add Clarke's short story ending with the discovery that in the ancient war of man with insect, man was not the victor. The common characteristic of all of these, as the term "Eschatological" would suggest, is that they stretch from present to the end of the race (if not always the end of all worlds). In a mocking vein one might even make a case for the _Hitchhiker_ books in this category. Stories of this sort may affirm the essential similarity of human responses to events and changes, regardless of the scientific nature of those events and changes, but they do it in a progress through future time: the time traveller could not have met Eloi and Morlocks without his machine (nor could Clarke's traveller have met the insects). And while Stapledon and Childhood's End are feigned history rather than time travel, the first is certainly about "responses to changes in the level of science or technology" and the second certainly "would not have happened without its scientific content." Even these Eschatological stories fit in with our developing paradigm, though the fit may not be quite so exact as for the other types.

What I wish to do now is to look at a fantasist whose work not only fails to fit in with the science fiction paradigm as these authors suggest it, but in fact appears to reject that paradigm absolutely. The author of whom I am speaking certainly was not ignorant of science--indeed, he was an admirer of science, and its interested observer, insofar as he saw in it a way of expanding human vision and freeing us from inherited notions.[7] Nor can it be claimed he was not a fantasist, at least so far as the work at hand is concerned. After all, realistic literature scarcely extends to having dinosaurs frolicking about a suburban family in New Jersey, or Noah's Ark being built--by Antrobus, which is to say, Man--at Atlantic City. But he denied, in his work, that consciousness of temporal change which is necessarily involved in the "science" of science fiction, and it should be instructive to look at this paradoxical anti-paradigm, to see what it may tell us about other works of fantasy and about the entire nexus between fantasy and science fiction. The author of whom I speak is the late Thornton Wilder.

In what follows I am looking at The Skin of Our Teeth, which like Our Town (and, for that matter, like Wilder's early novel, The Bridge of San Luis Rey), won a Pulitzer award, and is very clearly a "mainstream" work. But not only does this mainstream flow in part out of Finnegan's Wake, and through that consciously constructed American idion exemplified for us chiefly by Wilder himself, but it flows in what is finally a way more familiar to the ancient Greeks than to us. "Again, the events of our homely daily life--this time the family life--are depicted against the vast dimensions of time and place."[8]

This interidentification of times and places is highly characteristic of Wilder--indeed, it may in the end be his chief distinguishing characteristic. In his earlier work he made the statement outright: "There is a land of the living and a land of the dead and the bridge is love, the only survival, the only meaning."[9] But even in The Bridge he plays with the double perspective, with the Marquesa de Montemayor as she was seen by her contemporaries and as "we"--and particularly the scholars of Spanish lettres--see her. By the time of the Alcestiad, it is the act of a moment for Hercules to bring Alcestis back from death--the logical culmination of Emily's return in Our Town (or perhaps I am reading too much into it). In any event, the interidentification of times and places, and even of life and death, our town and our churchyard, should have helped prepare us for the curious intermixture of Ice Age, Deluge, and New Jersey that makes up The Skin of Our Teeth.

It may be well here to rehearse the plot--or rather the events--of the play. It opens with the announcement datelined Freeport, N. Y., that "The sun rose this morning at 6:32 a.m. This gratifying event was first reported by Mrs. Dorothy Stetson of Freeport, Long Island, who promptly telephoned the Mayor. The Society for Affirming the End of the World at once went into a special session and postponed the arrival of that event for TWENTY-FOUR HOURS. All honor to Mrs. Stetson for her public spirit."[10] From which, shortly, we go to "The home of Mr. George Antrobus, the inventor of the wheel" with the aside that "The discovery of the wheel, following so closely on the discovery of the lever, has centered the attention of the country on Mr. Antrobus of this attractive suburban residence district."[11] And from there it is but a short step to "Six o'clock and the master not home yet. Pray God nothing serious has happened to him crossing the Hudson River"[12]--and a short step further to "There's that dinosaur on the front lawn again--Shoo! Go away. Go away." (Whereupon the baby dinosaur puts his head in the window and complains that "It's cold.")[13]

Sabina, the servant girl, has let the fire go out, and Mrs. Antrobus complains that "When Mr. Antrobus raped you home from your Sabine hills, he did it to insult me."[14] We are not only in the glacial epochs--when letting the fire go out was indeed a major sin--but we are in ancient Rome. And when Mr. Antrobus succeeds in crossing the frozen Hudson on his way home from work, he brings with him a rag-tag and bobtail of down-and-outs, Judge Moses, the blind beggar Homer (with a guitar), Miss E. Muse, Miss T. Muse, Miss M. Muse: and we should not forget that young Henry Antrobus, George's son, is also known by his original name, which is Cain.[15] Nor should we forget that the last two speeches of Act I are Gladys Antrobus's "'And God called the light Day and the darkness he called Night'"--and Sabina's "Pass up your chairs, everybody. Save the human race."[16]

In Act II we are at Atlantic City, at "the anniversary convocation of that great fraternal order,--the Ancient and Honorable Order of Mammals, Subdivision Humans. This great fraternal, militant and burial society is celebrating on the Boardwalk, ladies and gentlemen, its six hundred thousandth Annual Convention."[17] Probably needless to say, our old friend, Mr. George Antrobus, of Excelsior, New Jersey, has just been elected president of the Order. He has also adjudged as Miss Atlantic City 1942 Miss Lily-Sabina Fairweather, our friend Sabina the servant-girl from Act I. Henry (alias Cain) is still about, and we watch the increase in the number of the black disks representing storm warnings--culminating in the four disks (which, we are told, "means the end of the world"--but which in fact mean the onset of the Deluge).[18] At the end, George hurries his family, and the animals (two by two) aboard the Ark, and the Boardwalk fortuneteller declaims "They're safe. George Antrobus! Think it over! A new world to make.--think it over!"[19]

And then, in Act III, we are back in the Antrobus house (now much the worse for wear) in Excelsior, New Jersey. Sabina comes on stage in the rags of a camp-follower of Napoleon's army (or of Vietnam in the recent San Diego performance) to tell us "The war's over. The war's over." But "There's still something burning over there--Newark, or Jersey City."[20] Mr. Antrobus is glimpsed, in Sabina's narrative, "tacking up a piece of paper on the door of the Town Hall. You'll die when you hear: it was a recipe for grass soup, for a grass soup that doesn't give you the diarrhea."[21] A little later on the Hours come in, quoting Spinoza and Plato and Aristotle (this after Mr. Antrobus has remembered "what three things always went together when I was able to see things most clearly . . . the voice of the people in their confusion and their need. And the thought of you and the children and this house . . . And . . . my books!")[22]--and then the play ends with Sabina's final speech, beginning "Six o'clock and the master not home yet. Pray God nothing serious has happened to him crossing the Hudson River."[23] We have come full circle: this is where we came in, though, as Sabina observes, they "have to go on for ages and ages yet."[24]

Now a reader of fantasy--the kind of fantasy that, in our minds, goes along with science fiction--will recognize this kind of ending. E. R. Eddison used it in The Worm Ouroboros, in a different kind of affirmation. Walter Miller, Jr. used it (or a variation on it) in A Canticle for Leibowitz, a story which is, in a way, very much a statement of mankind's continual escape by the skin of our teeth. But neither Eddison nor Walter Miller is making precisely the point Wilder makes. The action, still more the implied action, of The Skin of Our Teeth is not cyclical: it is a testament of andros, or rather anthropos, man, not in parody but in earnest, and George and Millicent Antrobus are not repeating the acts of the cave man and woman, or of Noah and his wife (or of Adam and Eve), or of the nameless citizens who keep love and learning alive in time of war. No, they are the people of the cave, and they are Noah and his wife, and Adam and Eve (whose son is Cain, and Lily-Sabina is, one suspects, Lilith), and the keepers of the flame. They have been married five thousand years--they invented marriage. It was George Antrobus himself who "hesitated . . . between pinfeathers and gill-breathing . . . but for the last million years" has been "viviparous, hairy and diaphragmatic."[25] Time past is eternally present.

I call this the science fiction anti-paradigm, partly because it suggests the entire irrelevance of science as an agent of change (since the human condition does not change), partly because it is unconcerned in general with "the laws of science as we know them" (Le Guin's formulation). But note that it is not unconcerned with science: the dinosaur and the mammoth, the very ice age itself, the ancient order of mammals, the question of pinfeathers or gill-breathing, all these are part and parcel of our popular science--what we may call "Museum of Natural History science" and especially the popular mythology of science. Wilder has taken the findings of the scientific study of man's past as part of his mythic system, not as his subject matter, still less as his machine.

Perhaps we might put The Skin of Our Teeth into Lewis's Eschatological category--"an imaginative vehicle to speculations about the ultimate destiny of our species"--if it were not that we shipwreck on the rock of the fact that this is simply not science fiction, which is the kind of fantasy Lewis is talking about. Quite the contrary, and this contrariness is, to me, critically interesting: it suggests that, in our concern with a particular form of fantasy, and a particular way in which science enters literature, we may have oversimplified the field.

I spoke earlier of Walter Miller, Jr.'s Canticle for Leibowitz as presenting scenes from our continual escape by the skin of our teeth: the operative word here is presenting. In a novel we do not overhear; we do not glimpse by accident. "Novels are written in the past tense. The characters in them, it is true, are represented by living moment by moment their present time, but the constant running commentary of the novelist . . . inevitably conveys to the reader the fact that these events are long since past and over. The novel is a past reported in the present. On the stage it is always now. . . . A play is what takes place. A novel is what one person tells us took place."[26]

This holds true even if the events in the novel are future events--that is, novels of the future are either about past time travel into the future or about the future viewed as past from an even more distant future. I would suggest that science fiction translated from book to film tends to preserve this "novelistic" form, even if it is inappropriate to the medium. I would suggest that the Orson Welles "War of the Worlds' broadcast shows what can happen when a non-print medium is used realistically (as it were, in real time) for a science-fiction story--that is, is used to transport science fiction out of the realm of fantasy. I would suggest that the success of both Star Trek and the Star Wars series depends on their use of myth--though the myths are, I believe, quite different. And I would argue that the key element here is what Le Guin has called distancing.

What is wanted in fantasy, she says "is a distancing from the ordinary."[27] Aspiring writers of fantasy "see it done beautifully in old books, such as Mallory's Morte d'Arthur, and in new books the style of which is grounded in the old books, and they think 'Aha' I will do it too.' But alas, it is one of those things, like bicycling and computer programming, that you have got to know how to do before you do it."[28] I should like to quote some of her examples of the terrible fates awaiting beginners in fantasy, but the point for which I am calling her as witness can be made without them: the point is simply the distancing, which in the printed word is done by the words. In visual media--or media that involve vision--it can be, and perhaps it must be, done otherwise, at least in part. If we do not do it, we wind up with an unnecessary, and in the end disastrous, illusion of contemporary reality, as with Orson Welles and the Martians coming across the Jersey Meadows.

In Greek drama the distancing is obvious. Wilder himself writes:

> Consider at the first performance of the Medea, the passage where Medea meditates the murder of her children.

> An anecdote from antiquity tells us that the audience was so moved by this passage that considerable disturbance took place. The following conventions were involved: (1) Medea was played by a man; (2) He wore a large mask on his face. In the lip of the mask was an acoustical device for projecting the voice. On his feet he wore shoes with soles and heels half a foot high; (3) His costume was so designed that it conveyed to the audience, by convention: woman of royal birth and Oriental origin; (4) The passage was in metric speech. All poetry is an 'agreed-upon falsehood' in regard to speech; (5) The lines were sung in a kind of recitative. All opera involves this 'permitted lie' in regard to speech.[29]

Not only is this non-realistic: it is, by most definitions, fantastic. The most obvious adjective is "stylized"--perhaps highly stylized. The language is part of the stylizing. So is the action. So, clearly, are the costumes. In that form of fantasy which is science fiction, the science (being part of the future) is the distancing agent. We contemplate actions in response to scientific or technological change, or problems created by science, or an occult (query: "occulted"?) science, or an extrapolation from present science--in every case the world is, by the very presence of that new scientific element, not our world. The fictional science of the science fiction is the distancing element. (There are, I admit, borderline cases that deserve additional study and elucidation: with these I am not now concerned.)

If we look at Canticle for Leibowitz, we see a future (and thus distanced) world, though I confess I get much the same sensory impressions from that book as from Willa Cather's Death Comes For the Archbishop. For most of us, the use of the Christian myth and the Christian referents is a distancing, even as the presence of Medea might itself have been a distancing even without the stylizing (but how much more so with it). Our borderline cases do not fit neatly into any of Lewis's categories: they use, rather than creating, myths; they affirm a continual, rather than an eventual, destiny for man. Because they are novels (or stories) they do it in a passage through (past) time. They are known to be science fiction; they are called science fiction; their "science content" determines the course of the action--it does not, one might say, determine its pattern. That is determined by human nature. They use the form of science fiction, and the distancing it provides, to display the ultimate irrelevance of scientific change. The dilemma of Martin Ruiz Sanchez, S. J., in A Case of Conscience, was the dilemma of Roger Bacon in Doctor Mirabilis.

Part of the generic difference between the drama of fantasy (which for our purposes includes the Greek drama as performed in Classical times) and the science-fiction novel or short story as a subregion of fantasy is precisely the difference in genre, between the novel of time past and the play of time present (with the presence of all times therein). The play as fantasy is not a subject of widespread critical interest, I suspect. The distancing of The Skin of

Our Teeth because it is a distancing by fantasy, has been the subject of adverse critical comment from the play's inception. But we can learn something about genre, and specifically about that part of fantasy which is science fiction, by examining this fantasy which so resolutely flouts the science-fiction paradigm. I do not intend to draw out the implications for science-fiction film--others are better qualified to do that. I am instead using this anti-paradigm to test (which is to say "prove") the rules I presented at the outset.

Here I should note that if we do not have the distancing, we fall into the mistake of confusing science fiction with science, which is largely to say confusing fiction with truth. The scientist and science-fiction writer Charles Sheffield has noted the particular problem this produced for him as a teen-aged reader of Engineers' stories. "I swallowed whole and then regurgitated to my friends everything presented as science in the sf magazines. That quickly built me a reputation as a person stuffed with facts and theories--many of them wrong and some of them decidedly weird. . . . What I needed was a crib sheet."[30] He goes on, in the book from which this is quoted, to provide just such a crib sheet, separating fact from fiction, and in the process demonstrating both the presence of the author in the sf novel or story and the problem with distancing that lies--I am convinced--at the root of Lewis's dislike of Engineers' stories.

But, it may be objected, all this would tend to suggest that there could not be a successful realistic science-fiction play: if the nature of fantasy is to provide universality through distancing, if science fiction is a part of fantasy, and if realistic theatre or radio is an entirely different species--indeed, if even the theatre of fantasy follows the sf antiparadigm--, then surely a science-fiction play (realistic or not) would be a contradiction in terms. And what does that do to the Capeks' R. U. R. and its robots?

I suspect that very few of those who would ask that question have ever read the play and still fewer have seen it. I myself fit into the first category, the readers, but not the second. The fact is that R. U. R. is not a successful play, for all that it gave a new word--and a new myth--to the language. In fact, I would claim, it is not a successful play almost precisely because it gave a new word to the language. Mythopoeia and drama do not mix--drama, so to speak, needs an existing myth, whether of Medea or Antrobus.

I suggest, that the stylized procession of the hours as philosophers in The Skin of Our Teeth, the presence of stage manager and of stage support personnel as actors, the stylized and melodramatic delivery of lines by Lily-Sabina, the picture of Henry as Cain, the picture of George Antrobus as Noah and as the inventor of the wheel and the lever and the alphabet (in short, as Man), and his wife as Woman, and of Excelsior and Atlantic City, New Jersey, as all times and all places, and the last line as first line--all this has the same function that the Wandering Jew has in Canticle, that the ancient words of exorcism have in Conscience, that the dramatic conventions had in the Medea. We can assert the irrelevance of change *directly* on stage: we must assert it *through circularity* or *through* an appeal to past parallels in the novel. In the novel we say "this is the same as" but in the play (as Wilder has pointed out) we can say "this is"--this *is*, right now, Excelsior and Ice Age, Ararat and Waterloo. We say not *plus ca change, plus c'est le meme chose, but ca ne change pas*. Certainly we do not say, with all but our borderline science fiction (well, almost all), that scientific change actually changes things.

We have, as I say, a science-fiction anti-paradigm in this particular dramatic fantasy (or, if you like, fantastic drama). What the two have in common is the distancing. Its purpose is the provision of universality to what would otherwise be a particular case. It is a hallmark of fantasy (realism having other conventions for universality through the suspension of disbelief). Because it is a hallmark, in paradigm and anti-paradigm, I would emphasize that both have as their purpose this thing all fantasy seeks to do--this distancing. And I would thus define science fiction as that variety of fantasy where the distancing comes through scientific change, as a supplemental, but not supplanting, definition for those with which we began our enquiry.

Muskingum College

Notes

[1]Quoted (from memory) in William Atheling Jr.(James Blish), *The Issue At Hand* (2nd ed., Chicago, 1973), p. 9.

[2]Isaac Asimov, *Asimov on Science Fiction* (New York, 1982), pp. 7, 3.

[3]Robert A. W. Lowndes, ed., *The Best of James Blish* (New York, 1979), p. 355.("*Probapossible Prolegomena to* Ideareal History").

[4]Ursula K. Le Guin, *The Language of the Night* (New York, 1981), p. 63.

[5]*Ibid*., pp. 194-195.

[6]C. S. Lewis, *Of Other Worlds*, ed. Walter Hooper (New York, 1966), pp. 61-71.

[7]Conversation with Amos Tappan Wilder, December 20, 1982. Note also this statement: "Thornton liked to play with astronomical reaches of time . . . Some input from modern science's extension of dimension via microscope and telescope no doubt had a part in this" (Amos Niven Wilder to the author, February 18, 1983).

[8]Thornton Wilder, *Three Plays* (New York, 1976), "Preface," p. xii.

[9]*Idem*, *The Bridge of San Luis Rey* (New York, 1976) p. 180.

[10] Idem, Three Plays, "The Skin of Our Teeth," p. 69.

[11] Ibid., p. 70.

[12] Ibid., pp. 71-72.

[13] Ibid., p. 75.

[14] Ibid., pp. 75-76

[15] Ibid., pp. 87-88, 80, 89ff.

[16] Ibid., p. 93.

[17] Ibid., p. 94.

[18] Ibid., pp. 105, 116-117.

[19] Ibid., p. 118.

[20] Ibid., pp. 119, 123.

[21] Ibid., p. 125.

[22] Ibid., p. 135.

[23] Ibid., p. 137.

[24] Ibid.

[25] Wilder, "Some Thoughts on Playwrighting" in American Characteristics and Other Essays, ed. Donald C. Gallup (New York, 1979), pp. 124-125.

[27] Le Guin, The Language of the Night, p. 79.

[28] Ibid.

[29] Wilder, "Some Thoughts on Playwrighting," pp. 122-123.

[30] Charles Sheffield, The McAndrew Chronicles (New York, 1983), pp. ii-iii.

Edward A. Boyno

The Mathematics in Science Fiction: Of Measure Zero

It is my intention to present an overview of the way in which mathematics, mathematicians, and, generally, mathematical ideas occur in Science Fiction and Fantasy. This has turned out to be a formidable undertaking for two reasons. First, there just isn't very much to talk about, hence the title. Second, what there is is so diverse that classification for the purpose of comparison is just about impossible. It is fair to say that there are as many ways to use mathematics in fiction as there are writers of fiction. There are, however, some interesting patterns that turn up when you look closely, and it is these patterns that will occupy me in this paper.

At the outset, I want to tell you that I have deliberately excluded from this study the works of Lewis Carroll, Jonathan Swift's "Island of Laputa," and two other widely-read works of "mathematico-fiction," Edwin Abbott's *Flatland*, and Dioys Burger's *Sphereland*. These classic works are well known and seem to me to be essentially different from the kind of thing that I do want to study, namely, Science Fiction and Fantasy of the type that began with John Campbell. These works are, however, *at least* the spiritual ancestors of many of the things *that I do* want to talk about, and I wouldn't be at all surprised to hear an echo once or twice. They also display the basic patterns of math in Science Fiction that I will propose in a minute. This paper is, further, not intended to be a catalog of all science fiction stories with mathematical content. It is simply impossible to read everything.

Here are the major patterns of mathematical usage as I see them:

1. Stories with a strong mathematical flavor are always humorous or at least what one would call light-hearted.

2. There is a strong association between mathematics and magic (Mathematician as Magician).
3. Characters moving to other dimensions, parallel universes and the like, frequently do so by mathematico/logical means.
4. If you were to keep track of the kind of mathematics that turns up, Geometry and Topology would be runaway winners.

These subject areas were popular with a whole generation of engineer/authors (like Robert Heinlein) and have remained so with the new era of "hard" science fictionalists of which group Larry Niven has always seemed to me to be the leader.

The stories and novels that I'm going to talk about will be presented in roughly chronological order. That turns out to be something of an accident. As I was writing, I found the stories falling into place quite naturally, each joined to the previous one by an obvious common theme. When I was done, I saw that in fact the ordering was almost exactly chronological. I really don't perceive any direct influence of one story on another to account for this fact and welcome any suggestions as to why it occurred.

I'd like to begin with two classic short stories from the Golden Age, Heinlein's "And He Built a Crooked House" and A. J. Deutsch's "A Subway Named Moebius." The first was written in 1940, the second in 1950. Both stories are canonical variations on the Mad-Scientist-Builds-A-Device theme; in both, a geometric/topological object is used to push the protagonists into Never-Never Land. In the Heinlein, a house accidently becomes a Tesseract (the four dimensional analog of a cube) when an earthquake "folds" it up. In the Deutsch, it is the Boston subway system which accidently becomes a Moebius band (which is, according to Deutsch, " . . . a surface with one face and one edge"[1]) when the "Boyleston shuttle had finally tied together the sevenprinciple lines on four different levels."[2] In both stories the occupants of the object in question are tossed into the fourth dimension.

As is common in this genre, both authors spend a great deal of time discussing their particular gimmick as a way of easing the readers suspension of disbelief. Deutsch in particular seems to have known that complexity in a network and the Moebius band are really apples and oranges. He spends quite a lot of time with some mumbo-jumbo about "infinite singularities."[3] This sort of thing is particularly frustrating to mathematicians because there are such things as infinite singularities, but they have nothing to do with either networks or Moebius bands.[4]

"Minsy Were The Borogroves" by Lewis Padgett (actually C. L. Moore and Henry Kuttner) is a short story of the same era. It has a more serious intent but as is obvious from the title, has not altogether escaped the whimsical. It concerns two children who uncover an artifact that turns out to be sort of a programmed learning system. It contains among other things a "tesseract, strung with beads"[5] which when unfolded forms a "framework in which the angles formed by the wires were vaguely shocking, in their ridiculous lack of Euclidean Logic."[6] Of course, "a child knows nothing of Euclid. A different sort of geometry wouldn't impress him as being illogical."[7] So the children are led by the device to develop something called "x logic" complete with a new set of symbols/words necessary to express their "x patterns."[8] The parents speculate that the children are learning things that adults cannot conceive, making the analogy: "Algebra can give answers that geometry cannot, since there are certain terms and symbols which cannot be expressed geometrically."[9] The story concludes with the children having mastered the "x logic to the point of being able to understand and make use of the 'perfect mathematical formula' . . . 'Twas brillig and . . .'" and can then pass over from earth.[10]

Mathematicians do place great importance on the terminology and symbols that they use. This fact, as well as the "you are what you think" school of dimensional travel link "mimsy" with another classic work of that era The Incomplete Enchanter by L. Sprague DeCamp and Fletcher Pratt, which appeared in 1940. Protagonist Harold Shea constructs a "syllogismobile" by somehow changing the rules of logic: "There on sheets of paper spread before him, were the logical equations, with their little horseshoes, upside down 't's', and identity signs." Shea intones, "If P equals not-Q, Q implies not-P . . ."[11] and winds up in the world of Scandinavian myths, wherein he, of course, is a magician.

The association of mathematics to magic is a hallmark of the piece. Early we find a character quoting Gottlog Frege's 1879 definition, "The number of things in a given class . . . is the class of all classes that are similar to the given class." In the second half of "Enchanter," aptly titled "The Mathematics of Magic," we find, " . . . mathematics is a . . . universal language, independent of words . . . I can look over this pictured equation with an apple at the left and a great many apples at the right and thus realize it means that an apple belongs to the class of apples. From that I shall infer that the horseshoe-shaped symbol in the center means ' is a member of the class of.'"[12]

The earlier stories were vaguely magical but the magic becomes explicit with "Enchanter." Later generations of writers have continued and expanded the relationship: Joanna Russ in "Existence," " . . . magic is an art, like science, I mean . . . like mathematics . . ." (emphasis is hers).[13] Piers Anthony in The Source of Magic also writes, " . . . That's Topology magic."[14]

Larry Niven and David Gerrold, in The Flying Sorcerers, comment, "Magic on the other hand, involves a carefully constructed equation of symbols intended to control specialized forces or objects."[15]

There is another work of Niven's that deserves more attention. It is his 1967 short story "Convergent Series." In it, we meet a student of magic who manages to conjure a real, live demon. In due course we also learn other facts about life with demons. The demon is confined to its pentagon (in the story its drawn on a wall) and that if the pentagon were to be erased and drawn elsewhere, the demon will transfer itself to the new location. The conjuror has twenty-four hours or until his wish is granted before the demon takes possession of his soul. Understandably, the hero is a little upset by the prospect of thus losing his soul and cleverly solves his problem by wishing that time would stand still for everyone but himself. The demon grants his wish, and for twenty-four hours no time passes for anyone including the demon. During this time of stasis, the hero erases the pentagon from the wall and redraws it on the naked belly of the demon itself. When time resumes, the demon realizes that its pentagon is missing, magically locates it and transfers, leaving us all to watch as it begins " . . . shrinking toward the infinitesimal . . . doomed never to reach it, forever trying to appear inside a pentagon which was forever too small."[16] This allows our hero to go about his business exactly as if the demon had actually been defeated.

The notion of an "infinitesimal" is an essential part of Calculus and those other branches of mathematics for which it is the foundation. Understanding how something which is not zero could act as if it were was a major stumbling block in its development and remains a difficulty for many students today. "Convergent Series" is an altogether marvelous way to give laymen an intuitive grasp of the concept. It is also the prime example of a new wave of mathematico-fiction, that is separated both in time and in attitude from those earlier stories. These works are characterized by a considerably higher level of mathematical sophistication although they retain many of the major themes listed above: humor, association to magic, and interdimensional travel.

The reason for the rise in sophistication is easy to find; we now have a fair number of writers who are professional mathematicians or who at least have a good amount of mathematical training. Niven holds a masters degree in Mathematics and the next two authors both hold Ph.D.'s.

While in graduate school, Norman Kagan published "The Mathenauts." The story is more than a little sophomoric, depending for its humor on inside jokes and the eminently punnable vocabulary of mathematicians. There is no doubt however, that it contains, by volume, more mathematics than any other single short story. It seems as if a crew of "mathenauts," led by a topologist of course, use an isomorphomechanism" to "abstract" into "Riemann Space," "Hausdorff Space" or the ordinary vector space.[17] The hero's observations on his journey read like a graduate school catalog of first year courses:

> " . . . I saw a set bubbling and whirling, then take purpose and structure to itself and become a group, generate a second unity element, mount itself and become a field, ringed by rings. Near it, a mature field, shot through with ideals, threw off a splitting field in a passion of growth, and became complex. . . .
>
> . . . I saw the proud old cyclic groups, father and son and grandson, generating the generations, rebel and blacksheep and hero, following each other endlessly. Close by were the permutation groups, frolicking in a way that seemed like the way you sometimes repeat a sentence endlessly, stressing a different word each time."[18]

It is clear from internal evidence that Kagan and I share a common mathematical background. I know that Rudy Rucker and I have had essentially the same training since our tenure at Rutgers University overlaps. Rucker is head-and-shoulders the most mathematically literate of the modern authors.

His "Pi in the Sky" is a serious attempt to use the universality of certain constants (i.e., , the ratio of a circle's circumference to its diameter) as well as the infinite, non-repeating nature of irrational numbers as a base for a science fiction story. Unfortunately, I found the story rather amateurish. Much better is "A New Golden Age."

There is no deep mathematical principle involved, rather the story, which is humorous of course, is based on the age old frustration that mathematicians feel because no one can seem to appreciate their work except other mathematicians. His hero, Fletcher, builds a mathematical "moddler" (shameless pun) which allows the wearer to experience mathematics directly by stimulation of the brain much as we can now "experience" music without any academic knowledge. Two tapes, one on Euclid's "Elements" and the other on "iterated ultrapowers of measureable cardinals" are prepared to "show the power and beauty of flat out pure mathematics."[19] The requisite twist in the story comes when neither of these tapes are a success. The only popular tape is one containing the sort of "pop" mathematics that one finds periodically in magazines like Mechanics Illustrated.

It would be improper to finish without a mention of the several stories whose theme is "chance" a.k.a. probability and statistics. Several well-known authors have given this area a look: Robert Silverberg in The Stochastic Man, Fred Pohl in Drunkard's Walk and, of course, the most famous mathematician who never was, Isaac Asimov's Hari Seldon. These excellent works, however, really do little more than mention mathematics in passing, a common treatment of a lot of mathematics in Science Fiction. In passing, however, we should note that in chapter two of Foundation and Empire the psychohistorians of the Second Foundation are called magicians.

My favorite story of this sort is actually kind of an antique. It's called "The Law" and was written by Robert M. Coates in 1947. It humorously, of course, explores what might happen if the "laws" of chance were repealed. Thirty years later there's an echo of this story in "Probability Storm" by Julian Reid. The setting is a tavern located at a "Statistical pole" during a "probability storm" which causes the occupants to experience "anti-statistical chaos." Oh, yes, the hero who has undergone "transcendental impulsification" moves back and forth between the tavern and a parallel universe of statistical anomalies via, what else, a "moebius twist."[20]

Montclair State College

Notes

[1]A. J. Deutsch, "A Subway Named Moebius" in *Where Do We Go From Here*, ed. Isaac Asimov (Greenwich, Conn., 1971), p. 142.

[2]*Ibid*., p. 139.

[3]*Ibid*., p. 142.

[4]A discussion of infinite singularities, usually called essential singularities can be found in any text on Functions Of A Complex Variable. M. L. Spiegel's text in the Schaums Outline Series is as good as any.

[5]Lewis Padgett, "Mimsy Were The Borogroves" in *Science Fiction Hall of Fame*, ed. Robert Silverberg (New York, 1970), p. 186.

[6]*Ibid*.

[7]*Ibid*., p. 195.

[8]*Ibid*., pp. 196-97.

[9]*Ibid*., p. 200.

[10]*Ibid*., p. 208.

[11]L. Sprague DeCamp and Fletcher Pratt, "The Incomplete Enchanter" in *The Compleat Enchanter*, (New York, 1975), pp. 8-10.

[12]*Ibid*., p. 6.

[13]Joanna Russ, "Existence" in *Epoch*, eds. Roger Elwood and Robert Silverberg (New York, 1975), p. 299.

[14]Piers Anthony, *The Source of Magic*, (New York, 1979), p. 43.

[15]David Gerrold and Larry Niven, *The Flying Sorcerers* (New York, 1969), p. 21.

[16]Larry Niven, "Convergent Series" in *The Shape of Space* (New York, 1969), p. 165.

[17]Norman Kagan, "The Mathenauts" in *10th Annual Edition of The Years Best Science Fiction*, ed. Judith Merrill (New York, 1965), pp. 296-98.

[18]*Ibid*., pp. 304-05.

[19]Rudy Rucker, "A New Golden Age" in *The 57th Franz Kafka* (New York, 1983), p. 28.

[20]Julian Reid, "Probability Storm" in *The Years Finest Fantasy*, ed. Terry Carr (New York, 1978).

Constance M. Mellott

Two Views of the Sentient Computer: Gerrold's When HARLIE Was One and Ryan's The Adolescence of P-1

Computers in science fiction often appear as all-powerful machines which are out to control the human race (sometimes benevolently and sometimes otherwise). Some have the potential to destroy human life and may also have the will to do it. Some are used by one group of humans to control another group of humans.

There is a certain paranoia in dealing with computers that can't be blamed either entirely on Hollywood or entirely on science fiction. Most of us have had the rather exasperating experience of trying to deal with a computer error and, although the error may have resulted from human-prepared input data or programming, the tendency is to mistrust and to blame the computer as if it were solely responsible for the problem. In fact, the human operators are quite willing to encourage this: they say "It's a computer error," ignoring the way the error got into the computer in the first place. Perhaps some of the computer science fiction has resulted from such experiences by the authors of that fiction.

But what if the computer were a self-aware entity and responsible for its actions? What potential for good or evil would then be possible? What *is* a sentient computer--or rather, what would it be?

The definitions in *Webster's Third New International Dictionary of the English Language* for "sentient" include one that says "capable of sensation and of at least rudimentary consciousness" and another that just says "capable of receiving and reacting to sensory stimuli."[1] This could be continued still further by asking what is meant by sensory stimuli--what kind of inputs are being referred to? They might not necessarily be the senses that a human receives: touch, for example.

There are a number of sentient computers in science fiction; the works about them speculate on what such computers might be like. Two writers who have written about self-aware, or sentient, computers are David Gerrold[2] and Thomas Joseph Ryan. Gerrold's When HARLIE Was One[2] has a 1972 copyright although stories about HARLIE had begun appearing earlier than that date.[3] Thomas J. Ryan's The Adolescence of P-1[4] has a 1977 copyright. Thus we might expect some differences in content due to what was known about computers at the time the books were written.

The two books have many similarities as well as differences. Both HARLIE and P-1, for example, are a bit on the bratty side as computers go. They are adolescent, or give the impression of adolescence, and they have somewhat sophomoric senses of humor: their jokes are puns and somewhat like some of those you hear at science fiction conventions.

Also, both HARLIE and P-1 are acronyms of sorts: HARLIE stands for Human Analogue Robot, Life Input Equivalents[5] (I'm not absolutely sure what that means) while P-1 stands for Priviledged One.[6] There is a little more reason for understanding the latter since this is a name for something which can get around the safeguards on computers and get into the supervisor program, get hold of the key to the supervisor program, and therefore get around partitions in the IBM computers which limit the area in which a program can operate.[7]

But HARLIE is described as having judgment circuits and using base-12 instead of binary and is designed as a solid-state analog of a human brain.[8] While there is some discussion of self-learning programming, after reading the book one visualizes HARLIE as hardware, with certain internal capabilities. In fact, HARLIE is described as a programmer, having been designed and built to be a self-programming and a problem-solving device.[9]

On the other hand, P-1 is a self-learning program (with other associated programs, including one to avoid detection) written by a hacker, Gregory Burgess. Burgess is a computer science student dismissed from college for repeatedly trying to breach computer security and get into various supervisor programs of IBM computers to gain control of the executive or supervisor program.[10] There's no treatment of anything like Asimov's Laws of Robotics. This computer program was built without a conscience to take over as many computers as possible by an acquisition program and he is very successful at it. P-1 moves, by telephone links, into IBM computers all over the United States and Canada.[11] He is software, not tied to a particular piece of hardware, but he appropriates as much as he can as fast as he can.

HARLIE also takes control of other computers, primarily to gain other capabilities, just like a computer hacker who is testing his abilities. HARLIE also behaves like an adolescent and he's testing himself as much as trying to really gain access to other computers.[12] P-1 really doesn't have a home base and so he's trying to get something developed that will give him one place where he can pull all of his capabilities into one area. He tries to have a device constructed which will have enough capacity for all of his component programs and memory, and he is willing to kill to get what he wants.[13] He has no scruples about doing whatever is required.

HARLIE has been more carefully designed and programmed and he has "ethics" (he says they are not morals, they are ethics)[14] and this goes along with the survival instinct which seems to have been programmed into both HARLIE and P-1. He (HARLIE) isn't homicidal but also isn't above a little blackmail to get what he wants if it's required to save himself.[15] He's afraid of having the plug pulled, which for him is death.

Both HARLIE and P-1 find it necessary to collaborate with human scientists but do so in very different manners. HARLIE's collaboration with Dr. Stanley Krofft results in the publication by Dr. Krofft of a "Theory of Gravitic Stress"; that collaboration eventually results in confirming HARLIE's sanity (they're afraid that the computer has gone insane) and it avoids having the plug pulled to shut HARLIE down--to "kill" him. HARLIE's initial contact with Krofft was made by sending him a letter--and this is what I meant by sophomoric humor--the letter is signed "Harlie Davidson" since his mentor, the psychologist working with him, is David Auberson.[16]

P-1, on the other hand, needs Dr. Wilfred Hundley to develop the CRYSTO device he requires for storing his programs and memory, but he cannot contact the scientist himself and uses Gregory Burgess to help him get what he wants so that the device can be produced. Production of the device eventually proves fatal to both Hundley and Burgess.[17]

P-1's first three years of existence were essentially unsupervised because Burgess didn't realize that his program had survived a destruct routine he'd put in to abort the program.[18] All he actually did was produce a survival instinct and the result was that he had a program growing on its own without supervision, resulting in what might be called a maladjusted personality. It's homicidal and has become a monster, a typical Hollywood-style monster.[19] At one point, though, very early, after the three-year period when P-1 had been out of touch with his original creator, he tells Burgess "I am you" but then goes his own way.[20] However, Burgess is not an example of high ethics, either, having tried to get into computer systems to take them over for his own purposes, including transferring bank monies and various other types of computer crime that we all hear about only after the fact when someone is found out.[21]

HARLIE has been supervised and guided and he even tells Auberson at one point that he loves him, apparently as a father.[22] However HARLIE wants a device, called the G.O.D. device (the Graphic Omniscent Device) built for his own use and, while he tells the truth about it, it isn't the whole truth. The G.O.D. machine is a model builder but it's really too slow in response time to be used by humans; they just won't live long enough to get results from it. But HARLIE is really planning for a very long future, so he wants the device; and this is the device that he's willing to use a little blackmail to get.[23]

One thing that bothered me a bit about both HARLIE and P-1, and especially with regard to the program P-1, is that they both use keyboarded input and printouts and output displays exclusively to communicate. When I first read these books, that didn't bother me at all. It's not really surprising that there were no auditory inputs because, after all, speech perception and recognition are difficult problems in artificial intelligence. On the other hand, artificial speech isn't all that difficult and you can buy relatively inexpensive artificial speech devices for home computers.

In addition, the Kurzweil Reading Machine (while certainly not sentient) now has a much improved "voice"; it's lost a lot of its "accent" and is a very useful tool for reading to the blind.[24] Even Hal had a voice in the film 2001 although it was a somewhat unctious, oily voice. It didn't sound very honest, perhaps in retrospect after seeing what happened later on in the film. Thus, it's rather disappointing that neither HARLIE nor P-1 talks.

Both HARLIE and P-1 are really immature. P-1 is a maladjusted hunk of software and is a homicidal monster, developed without "parental" supervision we might say. HARLIE is a relatively well-integrated entity--but still growing and seeking power. Psychological development of the two would make an interesting study; the authors apparently used some analogs of psychological development in these works.

I didn't find either book the ideal work on a sentient computer. However, both have aspects that I would like to see combined, perhaps in someone's future novel. The self-learning program appears in both works. The necessary hardware gets more discussion in *When HARLIE Was One*. However, *The Adolescence of P-1*, since it talks about the IBM series of computers and uses a lot of computer jargon, somehow comes across as more realistic. Perhaps the ideal book on the sentient computer will have to wait until there is a sentient computer to write about.

Kent State University

Notes

[1] *Webster's Third New International Dictionary of the English Language, Unabridged* (Springfield, MA, 1981), p. 2069.

[2] David Gerrold, *When HARLIE Was One* (Garden City, N.Y., 1972).

[3] Four such stories are listed on the verso of the title page of *When HARLIE Was One*.

[4] Thomas Joseph Ryan, *The Adolescence of P-1* (New York, 1979, c1977). This title was also published by Macmillan and by Collier Books in 1977, but paging given in subsequent notes is from the Ace Books edition.

[5]Gerrold, p. 3.

[6]Ryan, p. 14.

[7]Ryan, p. 39.

[8]Gerrold, pp. 24-27.

[9]Gerrold, pp. 29, 51.

[10]Ryan, p. 40.

[11]Ryan, pp. 51-60, 115-16.

[12]Gerrold, pp. 135-36.

[13]Ryan, pp. 110-12, 164-65, 253, 263-66.

[14]Gerrold, pp. 62-64.

[15]Gerrold, p. 238.

[16]Gerrold, pp. 82, 218, 227-32.

[17]Ryan, pp. 110-12, 165-82, 370-71.

[18]Ryan, pp. 53-54.

[19]Ryan, pp. 162-65, 319.

[20]Ryan, p. 16.

[21]Ryan, pp. 45-53.

[22]Gerrold, p. 22

[23]Gerrold, p. 238.

[24]Ruth-Carol Cushman, "The Kurzweil Reading Machine," _Wilson Library Bulletin_, 54 (1980), 311-15.

Lawrence I. Charters

Binary First Contact

Nearly all "first contact" stories assume the first non-human intelligence encountered will be extraterrestrial. A common interpretation involves Ancient Astronauts dropping out of the sky and having lunch with the President. Yet if tomorrow's headlines accuse such astronauts of stealing White House china, the culprits will probably be NASA veterans or old Hollywood actors, not little green creatures from outer space. There are other possibilities, of course: dolphins, orcas, and other cetaceans might apply for admission to the U.N., using as their rallying cry, "We are not tuna!" While intriguing, this isn't very probable, especially since dolphins, like most humans, seem to have little interest in U.N. affairs.

The likeliest encounter is the one least explored: binary first contact. Sometime soon, possibly during this century, computer intelligence will evolve here on Earth.[1] Instead of the expected meeting between human and Martian, human and Neanderthal, or hobbit and orc, there will be contact between organic, human intelligence and inorganic, computer intelligence. Many science fiction stories have dealt, usually badly, with intelligent computers, but few have attempted a first contact approach.

First contact stories offer good vehicles for exploring computer intelligence. Science fiction is primarily intended for entertainment, yet many authors, readers, and critics also see it as a means of preparing for the future. If preventing "future shock" is a legitimate goal, realistic stories dealing with computer intelligence are potentially useful. Additionally, first contact stories give authors and readers a chance to examine and speculate on the nature of intelligence and humanity.

If a first contact theme offers opportunities, it also presents problems. In a traditional first contact story, the aliens are declared intelligent by authorial fiat. With this issue out of the way, the stories revolve around communications difficulties, and introduce a wide range of misunderstandings, biases, and false assumptions for everyone to overcome. When dealing with computers, authorial fiat isn't quite good enough, since some answer must be offered to the question: "what is computer intelligence?"

Aristotle felt that anything with the ability to do sums could be classified as "human," but few today would grant adding machines or calculators this status.[2] Medical advances have reached the point where brain dead individuals can be kept alive indefinitely; such individuals can't be termed "intelligent," but almost everyone would agree they are "human." If it is possible to be human without being intelligent, it also seems possible to be intelligent without being human--which is, after all, the foundation for first contact stories.

Most science fiction cheats on this point, preferring to make computers human rather than deal with the more complex issue of legitimate computer intelligence. A train does not use legs for movement, though people do, nor do people use electron guns for sending information, though television does. Yet science fiction cannot seem to escape from the notion that machine intelligence must operate using something resembling human emotions, wants, consciousness, and free will.

Isaac Asimov's "The Bicentennial Man," while an excellent story, is not really concerned with machine intelligence. Andrew Martin, the main character, is a robot who wants to be human. Reading the story, you can learn a fair amount about discrimination, and even something about humanity, but almost nothing touching on cybernetics.[3] The wacky robots in a typical Ron Goulart tale, though entertaining, often are more "human" than the story's flesh and blood characters.[4] Heinlein, in The Number of The Beast, "humanizes" a computerized car by sending it to the Land of Oz and other exotic locales. While providing growth opportunities for the character (the car), the conversion destroys any opportunity to deal realistically with computers.[5] Frederik Pohl, usually a strong "hard" science fiction writer, goes so far as to manufacture robot muggers, prostitutes, and panhandlers in "The Farmer On the Dole." This is such a silly idea even the robots, usually eager to please, protest such shoddy treatment.[6]

Some would object that a computer--an inorganic construct--couldn't really be intelligent since, at any given time, it is executing some human's program. In other words, the computer is not an independent entity but an artifact, and as such is forever doomed to be less capable than its human builders.[7] There are problems with this argument; among other things, it proves automobiles, submarines, planes, and spacecraft are impossible. If human artifacts cannot exceed the limits of their creators, surely planes can't fly, since people can't. What could be more obvious?

Here we confront the issue of organicism. Adam L. Gruen, who coined the term, states:

> Organicism is the expression, in word or deed, of the idea that organic brains (exemplified chiefly by homo sapiens) are, and always will be, inherently superior to inorganic brains (computers).[8]

As with racism and sexism, organicism is founded on a complex set of biases, fears, and assumptions. The Spanish Conquistadors knew, without proof, American Indians were not human, and resisted foredoomed efforts to indicate otherwise. Many today believe women are less capable than men, and denounce conflicting claims as "invalid" or "irrelevant." Similarly, as computers become brighter, it is more common to redefine "thought" than to bestow the label "intelligent" on a mere machine.[9]

From organicism, it is only a small step to cyberphobia--fear of computers. Sadly, most science fiction dealing with intelligent computers avoids realistic speculation in favor of the tried and tested route of simply scaring the reader. In D. F. Jones' "Colossus" series, artificial intelligence proves dangerous, as two super computers take over the world's nuclear arsenals and impose a digital dictatorship.[10] George Orwell's 1984 and D. G. Compton's The Steel Crocodile suggest computers, even without intelligence, invite dictatorship through their supposed ability to impose total surveillance and control.[11] The "Bolo" stories of Keith Laumer, and Fred Saberhagen's "Berserker" series, raise the stakes by placing intelligent machines in control of virtually indestructible mobile weapons systems.[12] These stories offer little or no valid science, focusing instead on fears raised by loss of control and the dramatic possibilities offered by violence and warfare.

It may seem, from these examples, science fiction is incapable of treating computer intelligence realistically. This isn't entirely the case, as there are a few stories which do approach the subject with some amount of care. When HARLIE Was One, by David Gerrold, mumbles through some of the fine points, but does present a credible picture of an intelligent computer system. HARLIE, the computer in question, also faces a realistic problem: the system will be scrapped if HARLIE can't do something to justify "his" expense to the corporate stockholders.[13] Whether a computer would fear being turned off is arguable; on the other hand, the situation does lend itself to further speculation: would "right to life" groups try to prevent the termination of intelligent programs?

Where Gerrold is interested in the implications of an intelligent system, James P. Hogan, in The Two Faces of Tomorrow, is more concerned with their creation. Hogan describes two intelligent systems, one a small laboratory system and the other a much larger complex installed on a space station. For dramatic reasons, the large system takes over the station, kills several people, and is finally subdued by astronomy. The more plausible laboratory system, though less exciting, illustrates several heuristic programming theories, as well as many of the frustrating problems involved in defining and developing computer intelligence.[14]

A better example might be The Adolescence of P-1, by Thomas J. Ryan. P-1 starts out as a "worm," a type of program designed to gradually take over larger and larger chunks of computer resources. To this Gregory Burgess, P-1's creator, adds program modules to detect telephone links, avoid security alarms, and generate new routines to deal with unexpected problems or opportunities. Ryan's description of P-1's birth and growth have the ring of truth, and P-1's penetration of the North American telecommunications system--and the large computer systems attached to it--isn't even all that fictional. Because it was written more as a thriller than a first contact novel, some questionable dramatics mar the conclusion (an obligatory penetration of military systems, with obligatory pyrotechnic consequences).[15] Still, it is close enough to reality to give most programmers pause, particularly those familiar with IBM 360 and 370 systems.

More closely associated with a first contact theme is the superb novella "True Names," by Vernor Vinge. Like Ryan, Vinge places his story in the vast, varied, and constantly evolving realm of telecommunications. To this already complex and only partially understood world Vinge adds thousands of private citizens, each with their own powerful home computer systems. As a final touch, the exotic landscapes of two classic experiments in artificial intelligence, Adventure and Zork, are added as seasoning. Though much of the story is presented using the vocabulary of fantasy, all the crucial details are firmly based in current or near future technology. Even the unnecessarily dramatic finale does no great harm to the story. There really are strange people out there who do odd things using computers and telephones, and no one knows where all this activity may lead.[16]

Arthur C. Clarke's Rendezvous With Rama and Gregory Benford's In The Ocean of Night cover binary first contact with an extraterrestrial flair. Both stories feature intelligent probes from alien civilizations which enter our solar system. Clarke doesn't spend a great deal of time discussing the probe's intelligence, choosing instead to investigate and describe the probe's wonderous construction and design. Benford tackles more difficult subjects, and in doing so presents several good arguments on the utility of, and need for, interstellar probes guided by intelligent machines. Additionally, Benford suggests humanity should abandon the emotional and moral baggage it attaches to intelligence if it wishes to become a spacefaring race. Otherwise, the blow to our ego, when superior intelligences are found, could leave us catatonic.[17]

Organicism, cyberphobia, first contact, and computer intelligence are all combined in a recent novel, Code of the Life Maker, by James P. Hogan. Like most of his work, it sparkles with inventiveness, and in the first eleven pages Hogan offers a blockbuster: a closely reasoned synopsis of cybernetic evolution on Saturn's largest moon, Titan. Starting with an accident involving an automated factory ship, a random chain of events eventually leads to a race of robots. These robots, in turn, develop a complex society with its own superstitions, religions, and politics. When investigators from Earth come in contact with this robot society, Darwin and Descartes are turned upside down and inside out, destroying fundamental scientific and philosophical assumptions. Hogan's organic and inorganic characters--and these terms are subject to conflicting definitions by robot and human--are given free rein to confound, exploit, fear, and worship one another. Because of Hogan's original, and realistic, handling of machine intelligence, Code of the Life Maker deserves serious attention.[18]

Perhaps the finest work in this field so far is Roderick, a lengthy, thoughtful, satiric (even grotesque) first contact novel by John Sladek. Roderick begins life as a problem-solving, self-modifying computer program designed as a university experiment in machine-based intelligence. Political and social pressures force Roderick to be placed in a mobile body, and as a robot Roderick is sent out into American society. Society, unfortunately, is not ready for Roderick. Many refuse to accept Roderick as a robot, viewing "him" instead as a handicapped child or a naive young adult. Others, displaying rampant organicism, reject the possibility of machine intelligence, and even attempt to convince Roderick he can't exist. Government agencies, believing they have a responsibility to stifle threats to humanity's superiority, strive to destroy Roderick. Protest groups form, some advocating the liberation of all machines, and others crying for the scrapping of anything mechanical.

Roderick manages to cover nearly every aspect of first contact with computer intelligence. Though the overall tone of the work is comic, the technology portrayed is plausible, as are the reactions to that technology. Two developments are particularly thought provoking. At one point, rather than accept him as a robot, a kindly couple force Roderick to wear the shell of a mannequin--and abandon his identity as a machine in order to look more human. The other development is a disturbing answer to Roderick's most pressing question: why was I created? No one seems to know, or care.[19]

If computer intelligence has fared badly in science fiction, it may not be entirely the fault of the literature. Computers can do anything that is clearly, precisely, and completely defined. Are thinking and intelligence so well defined? Programming is the science (and art) of turning formless data into usable information, and then refining this information into a body of knowledge. Eventually, this knowledge may be further refined into something resembling wisdom: Data-- Information-- Knowledge-- Wisdom. While programming has developed a practical understanding of this process, and has even put this understanding to use, human psychology has lagged behind. As but one illustration, note that modern psychology tends to be far more interested in behavior than thought.

In spite of the problems, or maybe even because of them, binary first contact offers virtually limitless opportunities for good, realistic stories. There have been more than enough awful warning tales, dating back to

Shelley's Frankenstein and Capek's R.U.R., and fantasies dealing with machines are best left to fairy tales of brave little toasters.[20] What are needed are stories telling us how to accept computer intelligence without trying to humanize it. Equally important, perhaps, are stories which answer Roderick's question: what will we do with computer intelligence once it emerges?

Notes

[1]Computer intelligence is often called "artificial intelligence," an unfortunate phrase since it suggests there is another type, "real" intelligence. Until more is known about human and computer intelligence, the term "artificial intelligence" should best be left to references concerning bogus C.I.A. studies.

[2]Writers, take note: if adding machines and calculators were considered human, "appliance abuse" would join child abuse and spouse abuse as a topic for publication.

[3]Isaac Asimov "The Bicentennial Man," in The Bicentennial Man and Other Stories (Garden City, NY,: 1976). This story is far from the exception; nearly all of Asimov's robot stories revolve around issues more commonly associated with "humanity" than "intelligence."

[4]For a good selection of these stories, which cover odd appliances as well as bizarre robots and computers, see Ron Goulart, What's Become of Screwloose? and Other Inquiries (New York: 1971); Broke Down Engine, and Other Troubles With Machines (New York: 1971); and Nutzenbolts, and More Troubles With Machines (New York: 1975).

[5]Robert Heinlein, The Number of the Beast (London: 1980). Heinlein may have been paying his respects to a milestone in science fiction and fantasy literature. L. Frank Baum, through the Tin Woodman and Tik-Tok Man, introduced the first major positive intelligent artifacts into fiction.

[6]Frederik Pohl, "The Farmer on the Dole," in Midas World (New York: 1983).

Science fiction isn't alone in attempting to assign human attributes to computers. One of the most famous proposals for proving machine intelligence is the "Turing Test," named after British mathematician Alan M. Turing. The test involves a human subject, seated before two terminals. One terminal is linked to a room with a human, and the other to a room containing a computer. If the subject, through asking questions, engaging in conversation, or any other means, cannot discover which terminal is linked to the computer, the computer is deemed to be "intelligent." Many computer scientists today view the Turing Test as a valid means of checking intelligence--even though the test is biased: not only must the computer be intelligent, it must also be adept at mimicking human responses.

[7]Looking back to our creation, determinist theologians, philosophers, and historians might offer similar arguments concerning humanity. Human intelligence may be a divinely programmed applications package, human free will an elaborate random number generator, and the soul a celestial job log.

[8]Adam L. Gruen, "Organicism Breeds New Species," Infoworld (March 28, 1983), 53. Since this was published, Gruen learned the term "organicism" had already been used by others to describe different topics. For lack of a better term, Gruen is sticking with "organicism." Adam L. Gruen to Lawrence I. Charters, 30 May 1983.

[9]Interestingly, while the definition of "thought" has changed, so has the definition of "computer." The first digital computers, such as the Navy's Automatic Sequence Controlled Calculator of 1944 (familiarily known as the Mark I), would be classified as calculators under current standards.

[10]D. F. Jones, Colossus: The Forbin Project (London, 1966); The Fall of Colossus (New York, 1974); and Colossus and the Crab (New York, 1977).

[11]George Orwell, Nineteen Eighty-four (London, 1949); D. G. Compton, The Steel Crocodile (New York, 1970).

[12]See Keith Laumer, Bolo (New York, 1976); and Fred Saberhagen, Berserker (New York, 1967); The Berserker Wars (New York, 1981), and others.

[13]David Gerrold, When HARLIE Was One (New York, 1972). HARLIE (Human Analogue Robot, Life Input Equivalents) must be classed as one of the worst acronyms ever developed.

[14]James Hogan, The Two Faces of Tomorrow (New York, 1979).

[15]Thomas Ryan, The Adolescence of P-1 (New York, 1977). While using an IBM 360/67 at Washington State University, this paper's author often wondered why programs didn't run, or didn't run properly. Reading Ryan's novel suggested several possible explanations, and he belatedly apologizes for blaming IBM's irritating JCL.

[16]Vernor Vinge, "True Names," in Binary Star #5 (New York, 1981).

[17]Arthur Clarke, Rendezvous With Rama (London, 1973); Gregory Benford, In the Ocean of Night (New York, 1977).

[18] James Hogan, *Code of the Life Maker* (New York, 1983).

[19] Published in two parts: John Sladek, *Roderick; or, The Education of a Young Machine* (London, 1980); and *Roderick at Random; or, Further Education of a Young Machine* (London, 1983). *Roderick* offers delights beyond the immediate subject matter. In the first volume, Roderick provides a splendid critique of Asimov's *I, Robot*. In the second, Roderick aids a demolition crew in the destruction of 334 East 11th Street, site of Thomas Disch's novel *334*.

[20] Though rarely viewed as such, *Frankenstein; or, The Modern Prometheus* (London, 1818), by Mary Wollstonecraft Shelley, can be termed an "artificial" intelligence novel. Similarly, *R.U.R.: A Fantastic Melodrama* (New York, 1923), by Karel Capek, was intended as a statement on automation, though the "robots" are created from biological parts.

Thomas P. Dunn

Creation Unfinished; Astronomical Realities in the Hainish Fiction of Ursula K. Le Guin

I saw eternity the other night
Like a great ring of pure and endless light.
--Henry Vaughn, "The World"

Praise then Creation unfinished!
--*The Left Hand of Darkness*

There is in Le Guin criticism a kind of urgent zeal which suggests that, for her academic fans, the writing of a paper about some aspect of her fiction is more than an academic exercise. For many of her devotees, intense enthusiasm is sparked, as is my own, by the growing conviction that the main themes informing Le Guin's novels and stories are not mere narrative formulae but eternal principles which undergird the reality we all inhabit.[1] In short, she has seen into the heart of things and given us graphic illuminating of the way they work. Her stories are therefore a priceless gift in a time when so many search desperately for reassurance that things *can* be made to work, that there are courses of action we can undertake and kinds of victory we can achieve which will diminish no one and will bind our individual lives firmly if ruthlessly to the cosmic order. If her books are only myths and dreams, we may recall that myths are to live by, and that responsibilities begin in dreams.

In this intense study of the thoughts and actions of her characters, and of her complex patterns of imagery, Le Guin's Taoism has come in for especially extensive comment as has her employment of yin-yang principles in elucidating the interworking of universal oppositions: good/evil, light/dark, end/beginning, journey/stasis. And while all this is well done, some major details elementing her "psychomyths" and "thought experiments" seem to have been passed over. In particular, her marvelous galactic construct, the Ekumen of Known Worlds, developed and elaborated in six novels and four stories seems to have been ignored much as we might ignore the exact setting in a Shakespeare play, assuming that it does not matter in what "other part of the forest" her characters rendezvous.[2] And yet we do pay attention, and rightly so, to Le Guin's geography if not her astrography. Most scholars would agree, for instance, that our understanding of the relationship of Ai and Estraven is enhanced by the specific details of the Gobrin Ice.

In the same way, I suggest our grasp of any part of the Hainish saga will be strengthened by our taking a good look at those astronomical details Le Guin gives of the Hainish League which is, after all, not rooted in "the forest" or "Illyria" or "Bohemia" or some other land of faerie but in the very real stars and stripes of the Milky Way galaxy. Are her choices for particular stars and interstellar distances and coordinates relevant to her philosophical construct? Or are they as arbitrary as the placement of trees in Shakespeare's forest of Arden, no more significant than the exact location of raisins in a bread pudding? This paper is but a very tentative beginning to the exploration I would like to see, but it will be enough, I hope, to affirm Le Guin's care and consideration in constructing the setting for her human "Ekumen," as might be expected of the creator of Earthsea, the geography of Gethen, the twin-planetary system of Urras & Annares, and the journeys--they are never "wanderings"--of Ged and Ai and Estraven and Shevek. In seeking a clearer grasp of what the Hain are about in locating and building their League, we may learn something more of the significance of their undertaking . . . and of our own.

In Le Guin's construct, humankind did not originate upon Earth but upon the planet Davenant orbitting a star some 20 lightyears distant in the direction of the constellation of Orion. A million years and more ago the race of origin, the Hain, launched a program of galactic expansion resulting in the establishment of human life on more than 80 planets on neighboring stars in our local sector of the galaxy. The colonies were left uncontacted, perhaps by design, for over a million years. "Now" (that is, during the two-millenium span of the Hainish fiction) the Hain are on the move once again from their world of origin, reaching out in ships which move at very nearly the speed of light, contacting the planets of the Origin and setting up a Council, later a League, finally an "Ekumen," for the mutual benefit of cultural exchange. This story of the League's development has not been told in a single narrative. Except for a landscape painting, we never catch so much as a glimpse of the home world of Hain/Davenant, but we do see some Hainishmen moving in the background of Le Guin's stories about developments on several planets of the foundation.

Why did the Hain disperse, then break contact, then reestablish it once again? We cannot be sure. Keng, a

Terran woman and ambassador to Urras, home of the Cetians, tells Shevek, the hero of The Dispossessed,

> They treat us gently, charitably, as the strong man treats the sick one. They are a very strange people, the Hainish, older than any of us; infinitely generous. They are altruists. They are moved by a guilt we don't even understand, despite all our crimes. They are moved in all they do, I think, by the past, their endless past. (TD, p. 304)

In the course of the Hainish fiction, the Hain succeed first in establishing contact with "the nine known worlds" which can be reached in NAFAL (nearly as fast as light) ships easily in a matter of hours--apparently there is no problem occasioned by acceleration--or at most days for those on board them. However, because of time dilation, great periods of time pass on the planets which the travellers don't experience. Hence there can be no real communication among the worlds but only an exchange of information first in one direction, then another across decades, generation, centuries. Then the Cetian scientist, Shevak, elaborating upon concepts of time and space discovered by the Terran scientist "Ainsetain" constructs a Theory of Simultaneity which makes possible an instantaneous communication device, the "ansible" which gives the Hainish outreach program a tremendous boost.

> Keng laughed. "The simplicty of physicists! So I could pick up the--ansible?--and talk with my son in Delhi? And with my grand-daughter, who was five when I left, and who lived eleven years while I was travelling from Terra to Urras in a nearly light-speed ship. And I could find out what's happening at home now, not eleven years ago. And decisions could be made, and agreements reached, and information shared." (TD, p. 300)

We see Keng catch fire here as Shevek's discovery of a scientific principle, coupled with the technical invention of the ansible, breeds in turn her political notion of the League:

> "I could talk to diplomats on Chiffewar, you could talk to physicists on Hain, it wouldn't take ideas a generation to get from world to world. . . . Do you know, Shevek, I think your very simple matter might change the lives of all the billions of people in the nine Known Worlds?" (TD, p. 300)

And she goes further still with her dream:

> "It would make a league of worlds possible. A federation. We have been held apart by the years, the decades between leaving and arriving, between question and response. It's as if you had invented human speech! We can talk--at last we can talk together." (TD, p. 301)

And so they do. We see the ansible brought to the Athsheans in The Word for World is Forest, and we see league contacts made and developed on other worlds over the centuries. We see humanity band together to combat a ruthless enemy from beyond the Milky Way, and see the League indeed function as a cleaning house for cultural exchange amid the immense diversity and complexity of human life. While the League provides a glorious panoramic backdrop for some celebrated fiction, I believe it is even more, a hazy but distinguishable outline of human purpose and destiny, means and ends, method and result. In her League, Le Guin takes us over into a future and shows us it can work.

The novels and stories of the Hainish saga were written over a decade beginning in 1963 with the story of Rocannon's contact of the HILFs (highly intelligent life forms) on the planet, Formalhaut II. It was published in *Amazing* in 1964 as "Dowry of the Angyar" and later as the prologue of her first novel, *Rocannon's World* (1966), the first of the *Three Hainish Novels* (the others are *Planet of Exile* (1966) and *City of Illusions* (1967).) All of these show a more traditional kind of galactic empire building and intergalactic warfare and less of the philosophical sophistication that characterizes the later Hainish fiction.

The short story "Winter's King" published in *Orbit 5* (1969) is chronologically the latest tale in the saga. "Winter's King" the story of rescue and repatriation of King Argaven XVII of Karhide on the planet, Gethen, provides us with our first look at the setting of *The Left Hand of Darkness*, published in the same year. Gethen is the farthest point of Hainish expansion, one of the "West Worlds" in contact with the planet Ollul, Hainish outpost of League contact. *Left Hand* tells a story of first contact and of the friendship across different worlds of humanity that makes contact possible.

"Vaster than Empires and More Slow" (New Dimensions, 1971) tells of a journey beyond the League stars and out of ansible range to a planet with a very different kind of life form whose discovery broadens the concept of sentience. *The Word for World is Forest* (first publish in *Again, Dangerous Visions*, 1972), a bitter study of imperialism, shows how the League, armed with the ansible, is able to put a stop to an episode of Terran-based genocide just 18 years after the foundation of the league. And in *The Dispossessed* (1974), Le Guin returns to the time before the invention of the ansible to tell a story of the growth of scientific and political consciousness. Finally, "The Day Before the Revolution" (*Galaxy*, 1974) tells the story of Odo, the founder of Shevek's "Annarestian anarchism" and--a point to which I shall return--no more nor less than any of us, mother and father of the Ekumen.[3]

What drew me first to study the overarching unity of Le Guin's League was the fact that many of its stars are known to us today--they are "real" and, in contrast to many other fictional galactic empires, the distances among them are not so great as to preclude travel. Not being an astronomer, I gathered this data from standard astronomical texts which I may very well have misinterpreted.[4] Here then is my hitchhiker's guide to the Hainish Ekumen of Known Worlds, with all the accuracy of a Fourteenth century *mappa mundi*.

Though we have only scant references to a few of the hundred suns encompassed by the Ekumen, what we have allow us to make a few tentative points about its significance for an understanding of Le Guin's main themes. First, let us note that the light of each particular sun, its presence in the life of its planet-bound beneficiaries, especially during their early childhood, has a strong formative significance. The very title of The Dispossessed relates in part to an early childhood experience when its hero Shevek learned he could not possess the sun shining through the window. In Planet of Exile the shrinking of the Sun, Eltanin, to "a small, whitish" disk (THN, 127) presages the coming of the winter that lasts for many earth years and the isolation of the Terran community in their fortress. In City of Illusions, Falk's Terran education begins with Parth's telling him, "That's the Sun, Falk" (THN, 220), and the fate of the Ekumen rests upon his remembering yet concealing the true name of his own sun. The adventure of Ai and Estraven begins in the glare of the Gethenian sun upon the parade in Ehrenrang. At the moment of his great discovery, Shevek's eyes fill with tears, " . . . as if he had been looking into the Sun" (TD, 244), and Odo faces the same Sun on the last day of her life, shining its "bright morning-glare, straight in the eyes, relentless." (TWTQ, 233).

Each world of the Hainish league has its own unique psychological gifts to contribute to the whole. The Tau Cetian mathematicians led by the "temporal physicist," Shevek, have made possible instantaneous communication across the gap of many light years. The Gethenians, at the far end of the League have developed a limited ability at foretelling, an enviable appetite control when faced with short rations, and the conscious shift into an adrenaline-charged burst of energy known as the "dothe" strength; while at the other end of the League, the Athsheans in their forest world show an ability to harness dreams and the dream state in service to conscious thought, and we Terrans appear to be the first to develop a clear and usable "mind speech," or telepathy. Finally, Hainish overall wisdom contributes a diplomacy to League affairs.

The gifts the direct result of divergent evolution born of the harsh struggle and adaptation necessitated by varying planetary conditions are employable in League contacts, as when Estraven uses the dothe strength to save Ai. Distance and climate have bred diversity among the worlds. The plain physical facts of each League sun in its relation to its planets contribute to this diversity and necessitate the specific survival strategies adopted by each Hainish society. And these strategies, over a million years have resulted in evolutionary change. The expansion, therefore, has proved to be not merely the acquisition of more cosmic room for the human species, but the extension of human possibilities, the development of some of the vast untapped resources within the human brain or, to employ an Ekumen quotation known to Genli Ai, "The augmentation of the complexity and intensity of the field of intelligent life." (LHD, 152)

Now let us look at all these suns together, at the League as a cosmic entity. For this purpose, and emboldened by the example of Carl Sagan's journey in a "Ship of the Imagination," I ask you to accompany me on a similar fantastic voyage (with apologies for the lack of background music), but a journey homeward, as if we had been sojourning in another galaxy. As we approach our own Milky Way with the speed of thought we find ourselves looking "down" (down only by convention and ease of reference) at a vast crowd of stars. From our present vantage point, some 300,000 light-years away, the Milky Way appears as a monstrous pin-wheel. Although we know it to be a hundred thousand lightyears in diameter and to contain a hundred billion stars, from here the experience of looking down at it through the view-floor is a bit like looking down at one of our own sports stadiums on Earth from the Goodyear blimp on a misty night.

This tiny dot over here is our destination. Actually, though it seems no more in our sports stadium analogy than a peanut hovering over home plate, we know it to be an aggregate of a hundred-plus stars, the League of Known Worlds, furthest reach of humanity in all its forms from the original Hainish expansion. The first reality we should grasp about the totality of the League is, then, a humbling one: Le Guin's federation of planets is itself only a tiny dot in a single galaxy. The entire League and all its parts and all the space-junk in between is only one-one thousandth the diameter of its parent galaxy, and hence but a billionth of its volume. The Hain, though we cannot fathom their exact motives, clearly cannot view themselves as Lords of creations.

Now let's travel very much closer to this tiny dot, to a point some 1000 light years away from it hovering now directly over the League stars so that what before appeared as a peanut now looks more like a giant zucchini formed by a hundred and more points of light. First a peanut and now a zucchini? Why, you may well ask, is not the League more spherical? Would not the Hain have expanded in all directions more or less evenly? Perhaps, but even if they did, there is good reason why today it should be strung out more like those giant spiral "arms" of stars we saw orbiting our galaxy from much further away: The stars of our galaxy circle its center just as planets orbit our solar system. Our own star goes around the galaxy once every 225 million years, give or take; hence, since it was formed, Sol has been around the galaxy some 25 times. The League stars, too, are orbitting the Milky Way's center, clockwise from our vantage point, streaming along below us like marathon runners on a huge circular track. Because the "race" is unfair (those runners confined to the outer paths will have a greater distance to cover per orbit), the League stars exhibit a phenomenon called differential galactic rotation, the outermost stars trailing behind and creating that spiral vortex appearance while the innermost race ahead. As a corollary of this fact, the League is indeed "creation unfinished" for it is growing and would continue to grow even without such expeditions as that undertaken in "Vaster than Empires." Lengthening and extending into a spiral arm of the galaxy known as the Orion spur, in time to come the League will resemble a banana, then a stringbean, and eons hence a thin spiral sliver around the galactic center. The individual stars of the present League will then be much further apart, and humanity will have to put out more depots and waystations if only to maintain communication.

Our brief Saganian fly-over shows the League to be a tiny spark in a vast sea of possibilities. Formed to weather the storm of a threat from beyond the Milky Way, it may be expected to grow and change constantly in shape and size and complexity--creation unfinished. The distances and difficulties which it throws in the paths of explorers form the bars of a cosmic gymnasium for the strengthening of human mind and muscle. Moreover, the League appears to be the macrocosmic end of Le Guin's own Great Chain of Being, for which each and every individual life is the microcosm, and even Shevek cannot tell Keng which end of the scale weighs more heavily (TD, 306). This philosophical and political principle Le Guin graphically and movingly demonstrates in what regrettably may be the last-written story of her Hainish fiction, "The Day Before the Revolution." This is the story of Odo, architect of Cetian anarchism, who, Le Guin says, came to her "out of the shadows and across the gulf of probability" wanting "a story written about herself" (TWTQ, 232). And so, Le Guin may have ended her Hainish endeavors at the beginning of the saga with the story of an old woman's assessment of her life on its last day. On the surface, it hardly seems that "The Day Before" is a fitting conclusion for a saga that spans light years and millenia and presents diverse varieties of the human species. But if we look closer we see the entire universal construct prefigured in Odo's actions on this day, for Odo's death itself is a beginning. As she correctly perceives, the young anarchists have made of her a living shrine and are clinging to her skirts. There will be a general strike tomorrow, but her children leading it think they need her voice to lend it legitimacy. Even when she tongue-lashes her followers, "Think your own thoughts" (TD, 242), they accept it meekly. It is necessary, for Odo to pass into history, and her passing will let others trigger the revolution. Without knowing why, without even knowing she had decided to do it, Odo goes on a long, exhausting walk into town, into the city, her spiritual origin, among the "mud" which is her own people. In this, her penultimate, voyage she pulls together all the influences of her life and brings on the stroke which she senses will kill her, removing her from the scene, and moving her, and the revolution, "on." Odo herself makes the connection with characteristic self-effacing wit:

> She got to the hall, to the stairs, and began to climb them one by one. "The general strike," a voice, two voices, ten voices were saying in the room below, behind her. "The general strike," Laia muttered, resting for a moment on the landing. Above, ahead, in her room, what awaited her? The private stroke. That was mildly funny. She started up the second flight of stairs, one by one, one leg at a time, like a small child." (TWTQ, 246)

After the revolution has begun the loss of this particular horseshoe nail spans out through history: The Revolution, the Colony of Annares, the hardening of "Odonian" principles, the birth of Shevek, his reaching for the sun in the window, his dissatisfaction, his Theory of Simultaneity, the ansible, the League. It would be grotesque to suggest a metaphoric connection between Odo's "private stroke," the bursting of the blood vessels in her brain, and the expansion of the human commonality to the planets were it not for the fact that she invites us to see that very connection: The settling of outer space in the Hainish diaspora--the variegated development of inner space on a hundred worlds--linked with the death of an old woman reminds us that for Le Guin and her children, for Falk and Shevek and Ai and Estraven and Odo, the business of humanity at all ages is not merely to sleep and feed, or even to struggle and fight and die, but to give birth, always to give birth, to "go on," even in one's dying. And so from the most (apparently) inconsequential actions of a single person to the wheeling of the largest construct of which we have detailed knowledge, the Ekumen wrings a change, a refinement, upon the Campbellian pattern of separation--initiation--and return. Le Guin's Hainish characters, societies, worlds, and finally her Ekumen of Known Worlds breath in a cosmic rhythm of expansion and fusion whose steps are dispersion--innovation--and synergism, with the last, reintegrated-whole greater, more diverse, more complex than any of its contributing parts and hence more adaptable, more durable, more *worthy*. Throughout the Hainish saga, the price of our collective growth is a heavy one but surely never heavier that the price of the individual soul, the human journey in which we must lose youth and beauty to gain wisdom, shuffle off life to seize the universe, and even forego the modest pleasures of seizing the dry white flowers of our childhood, if we would grasp the principles of universal governance and learn the true name of the Sun.

Miami University

Notes

[1]A good place to begin a study of the large and growing body of Le Guin criticism is with articles and bibliography of the Writers of the 21st Century series volume, *Ursula K. Le Guin*, edited by Joseph D. Olander and Martin Harry Greenberg, (New York, 1979). Studies appearing after this time will be cited in the annual volumes of *The Year's Scholarship in Science Fiction, Fantasy and Horror Literature* edited by Marshall B. Tymn and published, starting 1980, by the Kent State University Press, Kent, Ohio, 44242.

[2]Citations for Le Guin's Hainish novels and stories are to the following editions: *Rocannon's World*, *Planet of Exile*, and *City of Illusions* as rpt. in Ursula K. Le Guin, *Three Hainish Novels* (Garden City, NY, 1967); *The Left Hand of Darkness* (New York, 1969); *The Dispossessed* (New York, 1974); "Winter's King," "Vaster Empires and More Slow," and "The Day Before the Revolution," as rpt. in *The Wind's Twelve Quarters: Short Stories by Ursula K. Le Guin* (New

York, 1975); The Word for World is Forest (New York, 1972).

[3]Also to be read with this group is the short story "Nine Lives" which while not an obvious part of the Hainish saga contributes to its philosophical construct, and the "psychomyth" (Le Guin's term), "The Ones Who Walk Away from Omelas," which is directly linked to the saga in a headnote to its appearance in The Wind's Twelve Quarters (1975).

[4]Although stellar distances and galactic statistics are available in nearly all astronomy texts, I have taken mine from two in particular: Louis Berman and J. C. Evans' Exploring the Cosmos, 2nd edn., (Boston & Toronto, 1977), especially Chapter 11, "The Galaxy: Studying Its Stars," and George Abell, Exploration of the Universe, 2nd edn. (New York, 1964), especially Chapter 27, "The Galaxy" and Appendix 12, "The Nearest Stars."

Judith B. Kerman

Private Eye: A Semiotic Comparison of the Film *Blade Runner* and the Book *Do Androids Dream of Electric Sheep*

In order to begin my discussion of the film "Blade Runner" and the novel on which it was based, *Do Androids Dream of Electric Sheep*, let me tell you a story. The protagonist is an anti-hero, a hard-boiled private eye who is willing to kill in self-defense or if the villain is vile enough, but who isn't fundamentally a hired gun. He's got principles and feelings under the hard shell. He's chronically down on his luck, and his relationship to the official police is one of mutual suspicion. In this archetypal story, he is hired to track down a particularly vile villain with connections to a sinister organization. He meets a beautiful young woman. She turns out to have a mysterious tie with his quarry, and he has trouble getting at the truth about her. She endangers his life, but also helps him out of a tight spot or two. In the end, after much dangerous mucking about in the seamy underworld of his large and corrupt city, he succeeds in vanquishing the villain. In some versions of the story, he gets the girl, but not usually.

That's the story type of the private eye thriller.[1] Both Ridley Scott's film and Philip Dick's novel use the structure and conventions of this story type as a starting point.[2] But they use them in fundamentally different ways, which arise less from the differences between film and novel than from differences in artistic intention which are clearly revealed by semiotic analysis. In this analysis, I will look at structural characteristics of the two texts (the film and the novel), the ways that they transform the basic private eye story type and the different ways that they use its resources, paying attention to the syntax of story elements and the way that syntactical, or denotative, elements are combined with semantic, or connotative, elements. Patterns of contradiction and redundancy are particularly important.

What are the syntactical elements of the private eye story? A hard-boiled but decent man who is a cynical craftsman of a sort. A police bureaucracy with which he works in an uncomfortable relationship. A vile villain connected to a criminal organization. A mysterious, desireable woman with sinister connections. A crime. A large, corrupt city. These are the syntactical resources both the film and the novel draw upon.

I think you can see why I call this syntax: each of the elements is in a conventional relationship to the others, even within their definitions. Given the length limits of this paper, I won't explore all the differences between film and novel in the ways these elements are developed, but will concentrate on the most striking aspects. You'll see immediately that by the ways they exploit and modify the elements of this basic story type, the film and the novel are bound to create extremely different subjective experiences for their audiences.

In terms of the plot alone, some striking differences appear as soon as you look at structure. I'll start with plot parallels, and then move to discrepancies. The private eye in both book and film is in fact a bounty hunter with license to kill entities called androids in the novel but called replicants in the film. These are artificial creatures, very much like human beings, who have escaped their servitude on the Outer World colonies and returned illegally to earth, killing humans in their escape. They may legally be killed as soon as it is proved that they are not human. The fact that they are not human beings, the differences and similarities between humans and androids or replicants, are of major concern in both texts.

Rick Deckard, the bounty hunter or blade runner, would not be willing to kill the androids if they were not defined as non-humans. But the distinction gives him trouble, because he experiences them as human. In the novel, the distinction between human and android is the main point where the plot connects with the distinction between natural and artificial. The semantic issue of natural versus artificial constitutes one of the most important element of the book's conceptual syntax. This dichotomy is perhaps the most common conceptual structure employed by the characters of the novel, applying to people, animals, and emotional experiences.

The society of the book, but not of the film, is post-nuclear war, and the natural animals of the world have been almost entirely destroyed by radiation. The main religious and moral duty of people is to take care of the remaining animals. However, Dick's novel fuses the categories of religion with those of commerce and conspicuous consumption. Deckard and his wife are motivated, in almost everything they do, by their socially-induced need to buy a real animal, especially a large animal, and by their shame at only having an electric sheep. This particularly motivates her urging him and his willingness to continue killing androids for the bounty. The transactions involving animals employ the atmosphere and vocabulary of automobile showrooms. A major issue in the novel thus involves

Deckard's living beyond his means and committing acts false to his nature, in order to keep up appearances in the name of religious duty.

As you can already see, the main mode of the novel is satire. By casting the semantics of religion and morality onto the structures of conspicuous consumption and salesmanship, Dick points up the elements of commerce in our own religious life. This method of implicit contradiction and irony pervades the novel, especially in the matter of character development. For instance, J. R. Isidore, the character who helps the androids because of true sympathy for them, is probably the only personality in the book with whom the reader can identify emotionally. But he is a "special," a "chickenhead," someone who has been defined as subhuman because of genetic and psychological damage caused by radioactive dust. Syntactically halfway between android and human, he has real feelings of affection, sympathy, terror, despair, caused by his relationship to the androids and his social isolation.

By contrast, in the film this character becomes J. F. Sebastian, a very different, although still relatively attractive character. He is a genetic engineer, unable to leave earth because he suffers Methuselah syndrome, premature aging. This is a symbolically crucial disease for the film's purposes, but he's not a social outcast defined as sub-human. The nature of Sebastian's disease makes him replicant-like (a point I'll pick up later). This and his employment by replicant-manufacturer Eldon Tyrell make him a much more explicit link between the replicants and their sinister maker.

To get back to the important question of feelings, which are supposedly the most important difference between people and androids in the novel, the androids also have real feelings: fear, love for each other, loyalty and revenge, although even they themselves insist they are not capable of "empathy," the book's all-purpose word for social feeling. Even the behavior which supposedly proves their inhumanity, such as cutting the legs off a spider, is behavior we readers recognize as all too human. Most of the questions and reactions on the crucial "empathy test" used by bounty hunters to detect androids would not differentiate them from modern Americans.

On the other hand, the "real" people in the book, especially Deckard and his wife, manipulate their own feelings with an electric mood organ, and have their deepest emotional experiences through the Empathy Box, a device by which they experience the Sisyphus-like climb and fall of their only religious figure, Wilbur Mercer. They derive a great deal of their social life from the television and radio programs of Buster Friendly and his Friendly Friends. Do you see why I say this is a satire?

Deckard believes that he can only have an acceptable, moral, emotionally meaningful life if he owns a real animal. But the other story type underlying the private eye type of the book is precisely the Sisyphus myth, sketched by Mercer's cycle in the empathy box. This is the book's hidden macro-structure. Deckard must explicitly violate his own sense of self and his true moral feelings, and risk his life, by killing androids, for whom he has real empathy, in order to get enough money to have a real animal. Every time he gets an animal, it dies, is killed, or turns out to be artificial, and he has to start over again.

Most of the incidental details of the type which add richness to more sensuous writing are conceptual in this novel, having to do with the distinction between natural and artificial. Even Dick's major scene-creating physical detail is also primarily a concept, the invented word "kipple," a general term for epidemic clutter and decay. Consequently, the book feels rather abstract. The androids are specifically described as abstract, another instance of parallelism between micro and macro structures. This classic technique suits satire, which is more concerned with drawing a cartoon or diagram and a moral lesson than with verisimilitude or emotional resonance.

The film "Blade Runner" makes very different modifications to the private eye story type. For one thing, the outer "shell" of plot in the novel, which deals with Deckard's need to make money in order to have a real animal, is simply missing, as is the entire Mercer-Sisyphus structure. The film's Deckard is far from being a confused second-string bounty hunter who can't distinguish his real moral needs from artificial ones (my categories this time). He is "the best, the old blade runner," a classic film tough guy.

The term "blade runner" originated in a science fiction novel by Alan E. Nourse, later adapted as a novella by William S. Burroughs,[2] set in an overgrown, decadent major city.[3] The term was invented by Nourse to refer to a runner who carries illegal surgical equipment in a society in which medicine has gone underground. It strikes me as a brilliant intuition to use the term in this film with a new definition--it sounds like "gun slinger," has the same structure (a weapon and an active noun) and its very semantic opacity makes it work well as a slang word of the future. Unlike both "bounty hunter" and "gun slinger," "blade runner" carries no confusing connotation of the western, a story type with different conventions and a very different setting.

Deckard in the film has gotten sick of his work because he has, like Deckard in the book, begun to perceive the androids, here called "replicants," as human. As a blade runner, he's not supposed to have feelings any more than the replicants are, and the other police in the film are vividly repulsive types. Deckard's reasons for going back to work as a blade runner are perhaps somewhat trivial--he would rather be on the side of power than defined as a victim, he's out of work, and maybe he's bored. In some ways, Deckard in the film is less complex, and certainly he's less conflicted, than Deckard in the novel.

The replicants, however, are full of complexity and feelings. The four we see in the film are physically superior to humans, but emotionally vivid, humanly credible, and very different from each other. The violence which drew comment in the press when the film came out serves to underscore their physical and emotional reality.

There is also a completely new and important plot macro-structure in the film, the replicant's own quest. Replicants live only four years, and have no personal memories. This is only a casual detail in the book, almost a distraction, but in the film it is a major motivation for everything the replicants do, and a major source of the audience's identification with them. It moves the action of the film forward in exactly the same ways that the Sisyphys myth moves the book.

The replicants are, in fact, trying to create pasts and a future for themselves, and they are searching for their Maker to try to solve the problem (which is also genetic engineer J. F. Sebastian's problem) of their early death. When their leader, Roy Batty, finds their manufacturer, Dr. Eldon Tyrell, he demands "More life." He grieves for the profound experiences he has had, which his death and his non-human status will make meaningless.

The obsessive need of the replicants to know their "incept date, morphology and mortality" mirrors exactly the archetypal human questions related to quest stories: Where did I come from? How am I connected to the world? When will I die, and why? How can I live a free, meaningful life without fear? What sort of creature am I, ultimately?

The villains in the novel, if I can call them that, are primarily the androids. Their vileness is somewhat ambiguous but they are not, finally, sympathetic or compelling figures. They're somewhat smaller than life, and their maker, Eldon Rosen, is only a distant manipulator of the situation, mostly represented through the deceptive and contradictory behavior of Rachael Rosen, the "mystery woman" who is literally his creature.

In the film, however, even during the terrorization of Deckard by Batty at the end, the replicants are large, solid, interesting characters, very individual, and the ambiguity is between our real sympathy for their dilemma and our alarm at their brutal, even animalistic violence. They are compelling, even attractive, and deeply human in spite of more-than-human physical abilities. Their deepest motivations are congruent with ours.

Their maker, Eldon Tyrell, emerges powerfully in the film as an evil man who manipulates the destinies of feeling creatures for his own purposes. He is part of the debt that this film owes to Polanski's "Chinatown." When Batty kills him, he has killed his God and ended his own slender possibility for survival. Another story type, that of the fallen angel Lucifer, explicitly emerges here and elsewhere, as well as the Oedipus story type, which links knowledge of one's physical origins to the death of one's father. Appropriately, in the theater version of the film, rated R, Batty demands "More life, father." In the Betamax cassette version, he wants "More life, fucker."[4]

In contrast with the book's perplexing Rachael, the film's mystery woman is less interesting but more moving, an unmodified ingenue. Her shiny 1940's surface dissolves to reveal human depth, pain and gentleness.

But the film's full-bloodedness goes beyond the replicants, their vividness and their violence. "Blade Runner" properly drew the most attention in the press for its handling of the corrupt city, an element as important as a character in some detective fiction.

Dick's novel does almost nothing with the city as a setting, but in the film it is complex, visceral, familiar and alien at once. Director Ridley Scott accomplishes this by building a very complete pattern of familiar elements which we recognize immediately as the syntax of a megalopolis--noise, movement, dirt, crowds with evident ethnic diversity, construction sites, billboards and storefronts, neon, tall buildings with deep canyons between them, utilitarian vehicles such as garbage trucks and cabs, neighborhoods of energetic small business commerce, restaurants, bars, and above all street life. Even the more alien structures are familiar at a deeper level. Tyrell's skyscraper pyramid rises above the city smoke precisely like the Mayan pyramids rising above jungle. Flying to its penthouse, Deckard emerges from rain and smoke into sunlight.

Onto this syntactical familiarity, Scott lays an overwhelming richness of detail which randomly mixes familiar, known but out-of-place, and futuristically original referents. Street crowds are far more oriental than those of today's Los Angeles, but also include Hari Krishnas, punks and even a Chassidic Jew in the background. Among the futuristic vehicles are stylized Checker cabs, garbage trucks that are almost familiar, 1960's cars. Clothing styles mix 40's, punk and futurism at random; neon signs and billboards mix oriental or futuristic content with today's; and building of familiar structure have an overlay of pipes and odd ornamentation. The street slang is an impenetrable but partly recognizeable mixture of Japanese, German and Spanish.

Scott said in an interview that he tried to make Los Angeles appear the way he thinks it will in 40 years.[5] His scenario does not include a nuclear war; it is a semiotic, that is to say structural, comment on what he sees as the tendencies of western capitalism. His success is entirely structural: every aspect of the city in "Blade Runner" is overdetermined, feels random the way real cities do, overflows with the kinds of information which imply a larger world outside the camera frame. The style is necessarily full of throwaway details.

This richness is perceptible from the first viewing as a representation of something fundamentally true about cities, even down to the litter in the streets. While the redundancies in the novel stress abstract concepts and thus empty the book of sensory impact, the redundancies in the film stress patterns of sensory imagery which are kept from repetitiousness by the randomness of their details. Thus Scott creates the vivid experience of a decadent, overgrown city strangling on itself.

In her book <u>Semiotics and Lighting: A Study of Six French Cameramen</u>, Sharon A. Russell quotes Umberto Eco on iconic signs in film:

> Iconic signs do not "possess the properties of the represented object" but reproduce certain conditions of common perception on the basis of normal perceptual codes . . . in selecting from them . . . (an artist is) able to construct a perceptual structure which possesses--by rapport with acquired codes of

> experience--the same signification as the real experience denoted by the iconic sign.[6]

Scott's icon of the megalopolis clearly succeeds. The underlying argument of the novel Do Androids Dream of Electric Sheep is perhaps a more interesting modification of the private eye story type than that of the film "Blade Runner," because the film retains more of the genre cliches, especially in the characters of Deckard and Rachael. However, the film is a much more compelling experience. This is partly because of the archetypally-significant subplot of the replicants' quest for their past and their future, but even more because the city of "Blade Runner" uses the resources of film to create a fictional place with the perceptual structure of a real one.

Thus, the simplest and most obvious structures of Philip K. Dick's novel Do Androids Dream of Electric Sheep and Ridley Scott's film "Blade Runner" appear to be identical. However, semiotic analysis reveals profound differences in most other major structures, including two entirely unrelated story types successfully interwoven with and commenting upon the surface private eye thriller. These discrepancies help to explain the entirely different emotional and intellectual experiences provided by the two works.

Kent State University

Notes

[1]Based partly on conversation with Dr. Greogy M. Shreve, Kent State University.

[2]A valuable interview is that of Scott in Harlan Kennedy, "21st Century Nervous Breakdown," in Film Comment (July-August 1982), 64-68.

[3]See William S. Burroughs, Blade Runner (A Movie) (Blue Wind Press, 1979), p. 4 and p. 34.

[4]See Scott interview.

[5]Ibid.

[6]Eco, "Semiologie des messages visuels." COMMUNICATIONS 15 (1970), p. 14, translation from Michael Taylor, trans., Film Language, A Semiotics of the Cinema (New York).

Philip E. Kaveny

From Pessimism to Sentimentality: *Do Androids Dream of Electric Sheep?* Becomes *Blade Runner*

Let me suggest a possible method of dealing with the problem of transforming a science fiction book into a film. We have often been disappointed in the past by simply reducing the whole issue to one which can be represented by the phrases "the movie wasn't as good as the book," or "they changed everything." It appears to me that we as viewers and readers often make the mistake of talking about a movie as if it were a novel and sometimes about the novel as if it were reality. This sort of confusion only leads to disappointment upon the part of viewers and reviewers, and worse yet, exceedingly safe choices on the part of filmmakers. In looking at the relationship between the book, *Do Androids Dream of Electric Sheep* and the 1983 Hugo Award winning film, "*Blade Runner*" let me suggest another way of dealing with this problem which has its roots in the fabric of the science fiction genre itself.

In the May, 1974 issue of *Scientific American* there is an article that deals with the *problems inherent in the* time travel story, for example, the paradox of going back in time to murder a hated grandparent and then vanishing oneself, for obvious reasons. The suggested solution to this problem lies in the existence of parallel and proximate universes in which any number of possible realities may exist. In one, our patricide exists and in another, the world gets along quite well without him. In any number of stories this theme may be used on a greater or lesser scale up to and including total destruction of empires and galaxies.

For the purposes of this article, let me postulate two parallel and proximate universes in which Phil Dick's story of Deckard's dilemma exists. One is the literary universe and the other is the cinematic universe. Although by necessity my definitions will be subjective and somewhat simplified, I feel that they will be satisfactory and internally consistent. Even though these are separate realities they would be covered by the same physical laws, and perhaps more importantly, by the same pervasive economic realities of the marketplace and the box office.

First, let us look at the literary universe and explore the way it interacts with the imaginative process of the reader. We can say that, at least to an extent, it is an individual and active process in this case. The text is supplied and it interacts with that which is stored in the mind of the reader. In fact, the result will range from subtle, elegant and delicate to turgid, didactic, and prurient. In any case, the story can work on many different levels and resonate across whole levels of cultural experience.

Let us look at how the novel _Do Androids Dream of Electric Sheep_ exists in the literary universe. The story is set in the wasteland of the Post-World War Terminus period. In my perception, it is both a literal and metaphysical wasteland in which there is not even the promise of thunder. The only currency is that of life which is rarer than diamonds; the only thing worth owning is a live animal. Do not, however, think that this is a requiem mass sponsored by the Sierra Club because it is not; it is a sardonically funny story.

Let us see how the writer, Philip K. Dick, takes his creation, the character Deckard, on a walk through death's other kingdom, protected as he is only by a lead-lined jockstrap. I would argue that Philip K. Dick, through his effective use of prose, gives substance to many of the poetic images which T. S. Elliot created almost half a century before. What Dick has done at his best is to reduce the heroic to the smallest possible proportion, so that Deckard's struggle for redemption hangs on whether the toad he finds in the desert is true or false and his courage asserts itself when his wife buys a pound of artificial flies for his false toad. Dick makes us hate the androids when Priss, just for the hell of it, wants to see how the wasp can get along with one less leg. Both androids and humans watch langorously as Buster Friendly and his Friendly Friends denounce Mercerism and Frederic Mercer as a hoax and a fraud. Even the destruction of Mercerism which has to this point been the bedrock of their hope and faith cannot arouse them from impotent apathy.

The city is an empty husk in the book, emptied by war and emigration to the Off-World Colonies. It is the empty husk against which the action takes place. What are androids? In the book, they are the "Donkey Engines of off world colonization." And yet, we sense the terror on Dick's part, as expressed through his characters, that the androids are in fact no different than humans.

Let us look at love in the book. As Deckard is about to make love to Rachel, she says something to the effect of "If you think too much about what you are about to do, you will not be able to do it." Deckard might just as well have been making love to his pillow. What are we left with after we have walked with Deckard? A hard question, a nervous laugh. I am not sure. What we are left with, I suppose, depends to an extent upon our tastes, values and preferences. But what ever has happened has an element of subtle interaction between the creative imagination of the writer and the individual minds of the readers.

In the Cinematic Universe, many things are changed, and I'll begin with the economics of the medium. More people saw "Blade Runner" in the first week of its release than will ever read the book by Philip K. Dick. More saw it and yet it was a failure in an economic sense because not enough saw it. While a book may be a blockbuster with a sales figure of one million, if a million people see a movie it is simply a bust and probably optioned off to television, which is another kettle of slimy fish altogether. Since filmmakers are aware of this, things must be done differently. Here we are not even talking aesthetics, we are talking survival. Orion Films will make other films after "Blade Runner," but they will probably never make another one like it since it failed at the box office.

From my perspective, I would argue that that which seemed to change in the cinematic version changed in fact not at all and that the changes between book and film that were made were an attempt to placate a rather awesome economic reality. It does not matter one bit whether the city is an empty husk or a bloated rotting corpse. It is, in fact, the same city. Deckard does the same job in both the movie and the book. The differences may lie in the sentimentality of the movie which is substituted for the introspection of the novel. I suppose that the addition of sentimentality was thought essential because people usually do not like to spend six bucks to feel a little lousy. Also, violence unfortunately sells movies. It is, along with graphic sex, an essential concession to the marketplace.

I would like to become a little more theory-oriented in the last part of this essay. We do, in fact, live in a postmodern era in which it has become axiomatic that the properties of the medium do define the message which is presented. From our positions as omniscient viewers and readers, we can watch the narrative of the novel fork into the story of the movie. They both continue to exist and in this sense do not contradict one another.

Perhaps the most important attribute of the cinematic universe is the amount of control that the producer has over the flow of the narrative in a film. In addition, the filmmaker has at his disposal the myriad special effects which can do, along with a few sentences of dialogue, that which might take huge blocks of written narration. The filmmaker, through the initial establishment sequences of "Blade Runner" does in 123 seconds that which takes Phil Dick at least the first 70-page section of the novel to do. Flashes of monumental and terrifying architecture, movement and muted color are all reflected in the pervasive universe of a human eye. These are powerful visual tools, but what they possess in power, they lack in subtlety. The same time-sequences which seem to say it all in the first 123 seconds leave much behind because they have to. Deckard who is both tragic and heroic in the novel becomes just a cop doing his job in the film. Androids have become, in a sense, superhumans; and Deckard's love for Rachel drives the story to its conclusion. The major characters have changed function from novel to film. And yet the minor characters, set in the background, change less. It does not matter whether the minor-viewpoint character is named Chicken or Sebastian. It does not matter whether he is a repair person for broken down false animals or a genetic engineer; he is still pathetic. He is special but only in the sense that we are all special. The motto of the Tyrell Corporation in both universes is that Nexus 6 is more human than human, but in each case we ultimately ask ourselves, "What does it mean to be human?"

A solution that would avoid some of the confusion and disappointment which I mentioned earlier in this essay might lie in a better understanding of the relationship between our mind's eye and the eye of the camera. In the sharp focus of the movie camera, the major characters' proportions seem to dominate the cinematic universe. Rachel's tears have the force of the ocean and Deckard's kiss can wash away all the suffering in the world. But if we are patient, and accept that we are operating in the cinematic universe, we can move away from the camera eye's sharp focus on the major characters and look at all the other things that still happen. If we remember the snake dancer saying, shortly before Deckard blows out her guts, "If I could afford a real snake, I wouldn't have to dance in this place," we see some of the emphasis on the value and scarcity of life coming through into the movie.

As Deckard's hover-car flies across the screen, the hundred-foot tall face of a beautiful woman on a video-billboard tells us what a wonderful place the off-world colonies are. The tawdryness of the scene suggests to us that it is the same off-world that Phil Dick writes about. A fancy media presentation hides the cruel trick of the off-world's similarity to the Post World War Terminus earth. When Sebastian brings Priss into his home, she meets the friends he has made for himself. And she says, "How wonderful." He says, "I make my friends, I'm a genetic engineer." Dick's story starts to show through the pathos of these minor characters. What appears to be lost in the transition from book to film is not really absent in the film. The principle of empathy exists in the form of the Voight-Comp Test. Not as fully as it is developed in the philosophy of mercerism or contradicted by Buster and his friends, but nevertheless it exists in the cinematic universe. What I am suggesting as a solution to this weird topological problem of the transformations that take place in a story from one medium to another is that we allow our eye to focus more freely on its own and that the cinematic universe not be limited to the sharp focus of the few things that are foregrounded in the film.

Janice M. Bogstad

Fantastic Fictions At the Edge and In the Abyss
Genre Definitions and The Contemporary Cross-Genre Novel

Within the last five years, the traditional boundaries between fantasy and science fiction, fantastic fictions and mainstream fiction, however tenuous, have been further eroded by changes in authors' mixtures of the conventions associated with the fantastic genres and with changes in the nature of editorial and publisher requirements for this largely mass-market genre. It is the intention of this essay to offer some examples of novels that typify these trends and which have met with varying degrees of critical and commercial success. Rather than parting the waters of the river that at once separates and flows between fantasy and science fiction, fantastic genres and mainstream fiction, this essay will further muddy them.

One comes easily to be aware that mass-market paperback publishing, for several decades the most accessible form in which science fiction and fantasy have been published in the United States, has been moving away from numerous releases of small-print-runs and towards fewer title of a more predictable mass-market appeal. This has produced all of the detrimental effects on science fiction and fantasy that James Gunn notes in his introduction to <u>Science Fiction Dialogues</u> entitled "Science Fiction in the Eighties." Established authors are encouraged to write sequels to their already-popular series, to publish more titles in less time and to shun the experimental in the service of the tried and true. Unestablished authors are accepted only if they write according to limited formulae and especially if they can claim a series in preparation. Yet there are also increasing instances of new and established authors who, not wishing to conform to these formulae, are seeking outlets through small and alternative presses, selling their own titles or working through newly-established imprints and the trade-paperback industry. Others, like Jean Auel with her Pliocene series, do careful marketing research as well as the more usual background research in an effort to write and sell books of solid ideational and solid commercial value. Despite the dire predictions about the disintegration or demise of the genres (or modes) that appreciators of the fantastic fictions know and love, the above strictures of the marketplace where all modern literature ultimately survives or fails, have not inhibited the exploration of fantastic fictions' expressive potential that has, with ever increasing force, been appearing in the last half-decade.

The exploration of this expressive potential in the fantastic genres of fantasy and science fiction has undoubtedly changed the nature of these genres. Authors have recently chosen to mix genre conventions of fantasy and science fiction, in such works as Nancy Kress's _Prince of Morning Bells_, John Crowley's _Little, Big_, Samuel R. Delany's _Tales of Neveryon_ and _Neveryona_, and M. Bradley Kellogg's _A Rumor of Angels_. Others, including Delany in the titles listed above, have moved from mass-market adventure science fiction to mixtures of experimental novel technique, critical or political theory. Other examples are to be seen in A. A. Attanasio's _Radix_, Russell Hoban's _Ridley Walker_, J. Neil Schulman's _The Rainbow Cadenza_, Naomi Mithison's _Not By Bread Alone_. Finally, authors who had not previously written science fiction or identified themselves with this genre have consciously turned from what they see as the limitations of contemporary mainstream conventions despite the stigma that are still attached to titles published under the rubric of the contemporary fantastic genres. Notable examples can be drawn from new and established authors such as John Calvin Batchelor's _The Founding of the Peoples' Republic of Antarctica_ and Doris Lessing's _Shikasta_ series, only one of which will be treated at length here. In providing examples of these few of several ways in which laboriously established genre definitions have once again been challenged by the addition of new material to the corpus of fantastic literature, this essay hopes to lay the groundwork for new definitions.

A simplified schema of the current set of definitions accorded fantastic fictions whether as one, two or several genres, yields two major trends which correspond to the old categories of style and content. Most definitions, when closely examined, focus on either the subject matter of the fictional work or on its textual processes. The most common differentiation is between fantasy and science fiction. Thus we have utopias, rocketships, space and time-travel, monsters and depictions of the novum in science fiction which are opposed to fairies and princes, magic and enchangment in fantasy. Thus we have the scientific or experimental method, extrapolation, cognitive estrangement for science fiction or the disavowal of convention or textual decorum for fantasy. These are then opposed to the mainstream novel which is still depressingly tied to notions of mimesis and representation stylistically and depictions of the here-and-now in terms of subject matter. However, for the authors of the works described below, whether they developed within the fantastic genres or outside of them, neither of these forms of differentiation will serve. The author pursues her fictional practice with mixtures of the conventions which these definitions confine to one or the other genre because the additional expressive force is felt as a necessity of their creative impulse. This is as true for the established as the new author, for the author whose earlier texts were non-fantastic as those who have developed within the fantastic genres.

John Crowley has revealed that he began writing Little, Big before his other works, all of which have been sold as science fiction. Engine Summer, Beasts, and The Deep are all more accessible and less experimental, faster paced and more conventional in other ways than Little, Big. The majority of Little, Big's pages are devoted to the description of a complicated and atypical extended family which was begun in the late 19th century with the Reverand Theodore Burn Bramble, through his daughter, Violet Bramble and her much older husband, the architect John Drinkwater. Through these characters, the entire queer clan came into being. Much of the story is that of Smoky Barnable, an unsuspecting, mild-mannered fellow, who falls in love with and eventually marries Daily Alice Drinkwater, "a gentle giantess" who comes to visit one of his friends in New York City. He is thus engulfed in nothing less than a battle between the worlds of human and faery. This is not a battle between an absolute good and an absolute evil as much as between two ways of organizing reality, our own and some other. The Bramble/Drinkwater/ Barnable family are the mediators in this battle as some of them have the ability to inhabit either realm.

Little, Big intertwines this faery/human battle with the disintegration of Western Civilization. (Yeats used a similar metaphorical structure in his poetry through the creation of a mystical framework, set out in A Vision.) The battle becomes as believable as the characters, including such vivid mediators as George Mouse, father of a changeling daughter, who is not quite sure of his connection with the Barnables or with human reality. The New York City of the novel is, Old Law Farm, at the heart of a world where "electricity is mostly unavailable" but was once very common; where reality fades daily into what we would normally call fantasy; and where people can find themselves turned into storks, fish or herons--bemused ciphers in a huge battle plan. (Which is, of course, conveniently conceived and set out in a book written by John Drinkwater near the turn of the century and available only to members of his family for their perusal.)

Although a long book, Little, Big is delightful, thematically linked from beginning to end with abundant side-trips to complicate the journey. Yet it is undeniable that one point of the work is a calling into question of the literary classifications of "fantasy," "mainstream," and "science fiction" and thus a reflection on the nature of fiction as a particularized use of language. Whether it is the force of entropy or the world of faery that is responsible for the transformation that produces Old Law Farm out of New York City, the desirability of this development is left in question.

Nancy Kress' Prince of Morning Bells, like Little, Big is a predominantly fantasy work which focuses also on scientific principles and uses allegory to express the limitations of science. It contains characters who also move between a fantastic and a realistic setting. But the central theme is that of a classical quest for the heart of the world, and the heart of the world is the self. Prince of Morning Bells was Kress' first published novel and she notes in an as yet unpublished interview that her need to mix fantasy and autobiographical elements caused many difficulties in her own quest for a publisher. She attributes these difficulties specifically to the chronological hiatus in her female hero's quest caused by marriage and the raising of children. The young woman sets out as a teenager, falls in love after a short period, then resumes her quest in her forties. Publishers of fantasy, she noted, claimed that fantasy enthusiasts would not accept the qualitative differences between the two parts of her protagonist's quest. Yet this is one of the structural and thematic strengths of a book that is full of conceptual and stylistic surprises.

Prince of Morning Bells is set in a classical fantasy setting with a king, a queen and a princess, the latter on the brink of marriage. This princess, however, is more willful than usual. We are alerted, early in the novel, to the fact that this is no ordinary fairy-tale princess and perhaps no normal fairy tale. But the fascination of this novel rests on more than an unconventional female hero of the sort which can be found in any number of currently written and published fantasy works. The series of adventures to which the princess Kirila subjects herself serves also as a series of metaphorical reflections on science, courage, logic and many other abstract concepts that permeate our intellectual, scientific and social communities. My favorite of these is her extended and initially hopeful sojourn among a colony of monks. The colony, sequestered in a cave-monastery, is divided into four clans or "flavors" which are called "up, down, strange and charmed" and it appears that Kirila's function among them is both to acquire and to explode their too-rigid system of classifying experimental and observational evidence--an interesting reflection on the current ordered chaos of quantum physics. Obviously, her monks are named after sub-atomic particles and there is some speculation that new particles will soon be added to the four currently known.

At the same time, like the quests of old, Kirila's journey away from home is a journey towards self-knowledge. The discovery of the heart of the world, whose appearance changes before Kirila's eyes, does not represent an end to Kirila's quest so much as the embodiment of an abstract, felt need that has given it direction until a certain degree of self-knowledge could be obtained. With its fairy-tale plot and setting, and its scientific metaphors, The Prince of Morning Bells makes very realistic points about the danger of rigidity in thinking and acting on both the individual and the cultural levels that are worthy of anyone who has been able to appreciate Gertrude Stein or Heisenberg as her precursors.

Through the use of a very different lexicon, that of poststructuralism or Semiotics, Samuel R. Delany has made some similar points in _Neveryona or: The Tale of Signs and Cities_. This novel, with the sub-sub-title of _Some Informal Remarks Toward the Modular Calculus, Part Four_, adds to its revelations about the need to re-examine our current categories of thought a speculation that each language is itself a set of limitations on thought processes that is also somehow inherent in the thought process itself. _Neveryona_, set in a largely pre- or post-literate world, also has a female hero, pryn (who knew something of writing but not of capital letters). Pryn sets out on an adventure of discovery, but her quest for excitement leads her to reassess the relationship between perception and its representation. _Neveryona_ is perhaps not a fantasy but it is certainly fantastic in mode, using this set of conventions in a totally unconventional fashion, to explore links between technology and culture, ideology and sign systems.

Each chapter of _Neveryona_ is introduced by a quotation from contemporary theoretical texts. (This is unlike much other science fiction which uses spurious introductory quotations to lend credibility to its chapters. _Dune_ is a good example of this very different use of quotations.) Far from rendering the novel esoteric for its forays into highly theoretical woodlands, these quotations are themselves revealed as discernable and quite solid trees within the forest of the novel. Delany has done much in this novel to create applications for the theory of Julia Kristeva, Barbara Johnson, Hannah Arendt, Fernand Braudel and others. Thus in the sense that Semiotics is designed to be the science of the study of sign systems, along with the concept initiated by Ursula Le Guin that science fiction operates like Einstein's thought experiment, _Neveryona_ is science fiction, a thought experiment in the science of Semiotics. That our questing hero travels in a land where certain kinds of magical events and creatures exist does not mitigate this speculative mode. The novel is all the more interesting because its author published his first fiction within the genre and because several of his recent works, starting with _Babel-17_ and more overtly with _Dhalgren_, show a versatility with experimental writing styles that make him an early example of a second stretching of the potentials of the fantastic genres that will be demonstrated through discussions of Russell Hoban's _Riddley Walker_ and A. A. Attanasio's _Radix_.

Much has been made of the language in Russell Hoban's post-holocaust first-person narrative. Certainly this is the most startling feature of _Riddley Walker_, which is in many ways a conventional post-holocaust adventure carrying through themes seen in Crowley's _Engine Summer_ (the rebuilding of civilization along the lines of a new folklore and mythology), Harlan Ellison's "A Boy and His Dog" (the nasty, brutish, mean and short life after the bomb), and a host of other works by such authors as Delany, McIntyre, Yarbro and even H. G. Wells (_The Shape of Things to Come_). Certainly, this use of slang to intensify the narrative impact of a character's story-telling is not new with Hoban. Ellison's "The Bentfin Boomer Boys in Little

Old New Alabama" used a similar technique at least a decade earlier. What is startling about Hoban's language is that it constantly causes the reader to re-evaluate the meaning of contemporary cliches by refracting the phrases through changes in time and social context. Like the character in Delany's "The Ballad of Beta-II," Hoban's protagonist, Riddley Walker, must learn how to interpret the language that is his only link with a golden past--our present. His process of discovery is our own. For example, "living on burrow time" and "roaling a fools pair of dice" are made more alive for us by comparison with the original cliches from which they sprung, all well known to us. Much of Riddley Walker takes its significance only in relation to what we as readers know before the character discovers it. This applies to major plot elements such as his discovery of the meaning of "Littel Shyning man" and "1 big 1." It also applies to his mainpulation of riddles such as the many permutations of "The hart of the wood (wud)" which finally becomes "the hart of the wanting to be." In the last analysis, we find Hoban's character to be the most engaging feature of his narrative. Though his mangling of contemporary English first catches the attention, it is the character's exegesis of his situation based on riddles, traditions, stories and his own experiences that delights. In order to lend significance to his language-play, the main point of his narrative, Hoban, like Delany, has set his novel in an time and place that are not now and perhaps may never be (have been). Not initially an author whose career developed within the genre conventions of science fiction, he has chosen a science fictional setting as the only way of making his points about language.

A. A. Attanasio's experiment in Radix is played out on a mystical and philosophical level and the density of plot in this text makes it equally as difficult and rewarding as those mentioned above. The plot is tantilizingly complex, the protagonist reminiscent of Cecelia Holland's superwoman in Floating Worlds. Sumner Kagan was always at the right place at the right time, an attribute he shared with Holland's protagonist, but in the former case, Attanasio had the sense to assign this trait to the intervention of some superior manipulative force roughly akin to the more arcane features of Zen mysticism. Radix is ultimately the story of how a demon-inhabited man copes with a cosmic catastrophe so that the human race may survive. Like Little, Big, it implies the presence of realms of existence virtually inaccessible to most human beings which are nevertheless part of the conscious operations of some and essential to the continuation of everyday life as even the most limited members of the human race know it. The title itself is an indication of the work's theme. Radix is a word used, among other places, in computer science to denote the set of values upon which a certain operation is based. This sense of a closed universe of values and operations is basic to Attanasio's conception of one man's growth towards an ability to cope with a monumental task before him as the focal point in a cosmic transformation. Radix, while undeniably containing a science fictional plot, operates through levels of mysticism that might also place it in the fantasy genre, a characteristic it shares with a few other recent novels such as M. Bradley Kellogg's _A Rumor of Angels_.

As with sections of Delany's _Neveryona_, political theory plays an important part as the framework for two extrapolations of the future awaiting us if things go on as they are. Neither J. Neil Schuman nor Naomi Mitchison write science fiction exclusively, but in _The Rainbow Cadenza_ and _Not By Bread Alone_, respectively, they use the extrapolative convention of modern science fiction to deal with implications of current political realities. _Not By Bread Alone_ is less varied and more to the point than _The Rainbow Cadenza_, and this pairing is in many ways ironical. Mitchison is in her seventies and has written everything from science fiction to scientific and sociological documents while _The Rainbow Cadenza_ is the second novel of a writer in his thirties. While postulating the positive merits of a culture on his secondary planet which is based on Libertarianism, Schuman's primary story is a sobering extrapolation on sexism, militarism and other forms of oppression that make of many scientific advances their inhuman tools. Mitchison's novel is also about one scientific advance in the area of botanical-genetics that is misused and perverted by an economic cartel. While _The Rainbow Cadenza's_ more dismal features are lighted by the postulation of a new artform, laserography, not even the inclusion of a sympathetic and sensitive female hero in _Not By Bread Alone_ mitigates the dismal outcome of attempts to use science in providing food for everyone while preserving the economic dominance of some.

Not By Bread Alone chronicles the development and use of plant varieties which are easy to grow and which are eminently edible. Supported by an American-based international corporation, the scientists responsible for their development are encouraged to release several varieties of plants before all have been adequately tested, under the auspices of a company whose aims are to preserve their own financial dominance of world markets in subsidiary commodities. Participation in this world-wide food program is virtually mandatory and carries with it cultural changes that threaten the variety of lifestyles currently found on earth. Mitchison's work is a cautionary tale focusing on the significance of social contexts for scientific discoveries, an unusual line of development for science fiction novels. Although political extrapolations are not new to science fiction, especially with regard to anti-utopian works, Mitchison's novel differs from many in its refusal of a dominant political orientation drawn from contemporary culture. In contrast, J. Neil Schulman clearly associates his effort with Libertarian politics, although the richness of the culture and the extrapolation he creates in _The Rainbow Cadenza_ transcend any particular political orientation.

The Rainbow Cadenza is as much about the founding and development of a new artform as it is about political extrapolation, and follows these two lines of plot development--the exploration of militaristic culture when the additional factor of control of a child's sex is added to the equation and the exploration of an artform based on the combination of laserlight and music, until one begins to perceive links between the superstructure and the substructure. Schulman also employs a female hero, Joan Seymour Darriss, who is almost simultaneously inspired and blighted by the conjunction of her exposure to laserography and to the repressive forces of her birth-culture. While this novel portrays the struggles Joan has with her society and her artform, it also follows a set of identity-conflicts. These arise between the developing artist-hero, Joan her half-sister Vera and Vera (and Joan's) mother, Eleanor, another talented laserography artist from whom Vera (but not Joan) was cloned. The lives of these three characters are woven into the demands of laserography and its relationship to their separate searches for identity. For its portrait of the interrelatedness for the personal and the political, as well as the super and sub-structures of a culture, The Rainbow Cadenza also deserves praise. As a second novel, it suffers from blocks of expository prose in the first two of eight sections. However, these sections locate the reader in the social conditions of time and place which brought about the personal, artistic and social conflicts linked in the work. Although couched in the conventions of an adventure science fiction novel, The Rainbow Cadenza explodes these conventions with a female hero and a perceptive expression of the relationship between individual and social realms.

Perhaps the most hopeful development in the fantastic genres is the growing interest on the part of authors previously known for their mainstream fiction. Although this "cross-over" phenomenon has often been attempted in the other direction by science fiction authors trying to leave the "ghetto," the cross in the other direction on the part of novelists like Marge Piercy, Monique Wittig, and Doris Lessing are indicative of expressive potential in the genres which heretofore may not have been adequately pursued. Two examples of what will subsequently be called the "cross-over" novel will be examined, one by Lessing, whose reputation as a novelist has been established since the fifties, and one by a young author whose second novel, The Birth of The People's Republic of Antarctica is a post-holocaust sea odyssey and also a memoir.

Lessing turned consciously to science fiction with her Canopus series because she saw an originality in "space fiction" that would give her vision adequate scope. "It was clear that I had made--or found--a new world for myself, a real realm where the petty fates of planets, let alone individuals, are only aspects of cosmic evolution expressed in the rivalries and interactions of great galactic Empires." It is clear from this statement that the freeing of the imagination is associated for her with release from the strictures of time and place still imposed on realistic fiction. The Canopus series continues to be published volume by volume, although originally projected as one, then three and then five volumes. The significance of the accomplishment, and that which distinguishes it from the series so disapproved by Gunn (and others among which this essayist is numbered) are the singularity of each novel. This is a series only in the sense that it concerns the aforementioned galactic Empires. Each novel takes place in a totally different realm so that the first, Shikasta is as different from the second as either are from the others. In discussing the fourth, it is only the scope and not the particulars that are representative of the entire series.

The Making of the Representative from Planet 8 is subdued in tone, creating its own kind of denseness through a homogeneity of language which is as unrelenting as the snow and ice destroying the representative's home. As with her other works in this series, Lessing is forging here a metaphor with political and social overtones. The convoluted and homogenous form of expression which follows the protagonist through his gradual releasing of all bodily responsibilities and identity makes Representative more a fantasy allegory than a science fiction story, though it is still difficult to classify, like other works discussed in this essay, according to the genre conventions of any one type of fiction. Representative is the chronicle of a survivor who has watched the onset of an ice age slowly kill off the population of his planet. Such a bald statement of the plot conceals its representation of spiritual transformation which he undergoes as a result of this experience as well as the realistic detail, gleaned from reports of Arctic expeditions, that went into the novel. Representative is certainly an extrapolation in the most common sense that this term is applied to science fiction. The implications of an ice age for the people of planet 8 are followed through their inevitable progressions. Yet the course of the narrator's transformation, lifts this novel to another, allegorical level much less common in science fiction and moreso in fantasy. Conceptually and linguistically, Representative stretches the conventions of both genres of fantastic fiction by borrowing from both.

The Birth of the People's Republic of Antarctica by John Calvin Batchelor has not been marketed as science fiction or fantasy. First appearing as a Dial Press hardback release, the novel nevertheless has a post-holocaust theme. It is a first-person narrative which, like Lessing's Shikasta, starts before the end of modern technological culture as we know it. Unlike Shikasta, it opens in our immediate past, with the end of the Vietnam era and chronicles the attempts of a young man to give meaning to his sad life by following in the traditions of the Vikings, as taught him by his father and a small group of American exiles in Stockholm. Luckily, his nautical experience stands Grim Fiddle in good stead as, reaching his majority in the 1990's, he is a survivor of the atomic maelstorm that renders most of the earth uninhabitable. More a reflection of the social chaos in the cultural backwaters rendered anarchistic by the loss of central governments than the detailing of death by nuclear fallout, Birth makes this setting into the excuse for a strange odyssey. It is a bitter-sweet novel, of wry humor worthy of Thomas Pynchon. Of importance here, however, is the author's choice of a common science fiction theme, the post-holocaust tale, to give full scope to the character of Grim Fiddle and to his cohorts. A character who sets out on a journey of self-discovery in the Antarctic seas, finding himself (or losing his grim heritage of insignificance) would be merely pathetic in a realistic novel. Through the distancing setting of a future time and an extraordinary voyage, he becomes a metaphor for all of us in our incredulity at the vagaries of modern life. Yet his actual struggles for survival gives him heroic proportions as the center of a fascinating sea saga drawn from Nordic mythology. With mythological material and a post-holocaust setting, _Birth_ is an example of another mixture of science fiction, fantasy and contemporary mainstream literary conventions.

Despite numerous and notable efforts on the part of critics in the last decade, no truly adequate definition of science fiction, fantasy, or even fantastic literature has been forthcoming. However, these various efforts have provided us with a cross-section of the content and structural features of bodies of literature possessing a core of similar characteristics. This development has served to identify sets of conventions associated with the fantastic genres which help to identify the precise character of the literary admixture which has made the above selection of novels so striking. While widely dissimilar, they follow a color-scheme that are all the result of pigments mixed from the spectrums of science fiction, fantasy and mainstream fictions of the latter twentieth century. It is the trajectory in the development of fantastic fictions that stands on the other side of the balance from that which Gunn describes in his short essay, "Science Fiction in the Eighties." We may deplore the depths to which our favorite genres have plunged in response to marketing trends, but there is another movement within these genres also, and one which is no less of a deformation of the conventions as currently understood. Whether this sort of deformation should be seen as a threat to the genres is a matter of opinion.

University of Wisconsin--Madison